Neet,

from your

Planting Companion-

Mary .

1991

COMPANION
PLANTING

COMPANION PLANTING

RICHARD BIRD

NEW
BURLINGTON
BOOKS

A QUARTO BOOK

Published by New Burlington Books
6 Blundell Street
London N7 9BH

Exclusive to Coles in Canada

ISBN 1 85348 290 0

This book was designed and produced by
Quarto Publishing plc
6 Blundell Street
London N7 9BH

Senior Editor Kate Kirby
Editor Carol Hupping

Designer Anne Fisher

Picture Researcher Susan Rose-Smith
Illustrators Kevin Maddison, Jim Robins, Anne Savage,
Valerie Price, David Kemp

Garden plans Jane Fowles

Art Director Moira Clinch
Assistant Art Director Chloë Alexander
Editorial Director Carolyn King

Typeset by Ampersand Typesetting
(Bournemouth) Limited
Manufactured in Hong Kong by Regent Publishing
Services Ltd
Printed in Hong Kong by Leefung Asco Printers Ltd

FOREWORD

Companion planting is nothing new. It is an extension of what has been practiced by generations of gardeners before the widespread use of chemicals. Its aim is simply to provide the best environment for growing vegetables and flowers by selecting the correct plants as neighbors.

Over the years, as gardeners experimented with companion planting, they discovered that certain plants deterred specific pests and weeds on the land around them. Some plants served their neighbors, while others appeared to have detrimental effects on them. It was also known that a mixed planting helped to keep pests and predators in balance. On the whole it is this balance which is important, and there is no need for the wholesale destruction of all insects, good and bad.

Much of the information that is available on companion planting comes from gardening traditions and lore. Naturally it has been scoffed at by those who are wedded to the use of chemicals but, as with most traditional practices, there is a lot of substance in its claims. Scientific research has been neglected until recent times, but now more work is being undertaken particularly in the field of agriculture, where similar techniques have been practiced.

This research is already coming up with interesting results, proving that some of the claims can be substantiated. There is a lot more work to be done, especially in choosing the right companions to combat pests, and here the reader can help by trying his own experiments with likely combinations of plants.

It is not only live plants that can be beneficial; dead ones in the form of compost or green manure can help structure the soil and provide valuable nutrients without recourse to chemical fertilizers.

The companionship of plants is not restricted to the way plants can be used to look after and provide for one another; there are several other relationships between them that are to their mutual benefit. They can be used to physically support or protect each other or to complement or contrast with each other in visual terms, such as color, shape, and texture. These are well worn paths, but there is still a lot to be learned, and successful gardening depends on its visual qualities as well as its productive ones.

This book, then, is about the way plants relate to plants. It is hoped that the methods and suggestions it makes will lead to a better understanding of a natural way of gardening and that the reader will enjoy both rediscovering and pioneering techniques.

Richard Bird

CONTENTS

*I*NTRODUCTION

Human beings have had a long association with plants, but
plants have had an even longer association with each other. In
order to get the best from vegetables, herbs, fruit, and
flowering plants, it is important to have a commonsense
approach as to how they should be arranged in the garden.
There are many aspects to companionable planting, including
the mixing of vegetables and flowers in the same bed (*left*).

GOOD COMPANIONS MAKE
GOOD GARDENS

Companion planting, the gardening technique that carefully chooses and grows compatible plants with one another for their mutual benefit, is enjoying a revival. It began centuries ago in European cottage gardens but now can be found all over the world – in vegetable gardens, in flower borders, and in gardens that are delightful mixtures of all sorts of edible and ornamental plants growing happily together: vegetables with fruits, flowers, herbs, trees, and shrubs.

As you will hopefully discover as you read along, there are many good reasons for the present popularity of the companion garden. Plants can and do help each other keep insect pests in check. A mixture of plants that have different tolerances to diseases lowers the risk that a virus or bacteria will do much damage to a garden.

Keeping the ground covered with closely growing plants gives weeds little space to grow and protects the soil from drought and driving rain. And it makes the most use of what garden space is available. Climbing plants have others to support them, and weak-stemmed plants are better sheltered from wind if there are sturdier plants close by. Certain plants – "green manures," as they are called – use their long roots to draw up nutrients deep down in the soil; then they make these nutrients available to other plants when they themselves are cut down and tilled back into the soil. Other plants called legumes "fix" nitrogen directly from the air, making it usable by plants later planted in that same plot.

In addition to such practical benefits, a profusion of pleasing shapes, textures, and colors is a beautiful sight. If the companion garden is planned to respond to all the seasons, there will be flowers from spring to summer, through fall and possibly even winter. Spring bulbs like *Hyacinthus*, *Fritillaria*, and tulips (*Tulipa*) planted among herbaceous plants will flower before the others bloom. Then the herbaceous blooms do their part, hiding the bulbs' fading flowers and wilting greenery beneath their finery. Fall blooms such as those of *Aster* can brighten up a gap left by the summer flowers like lilies (*Lilium*). Ornamental grasses, even though they turn brown in fall, stand right through the winter, giving striking shape and texture to what might otherwise be a bland landscape. In areas with mild winters, the winter-flowering hellebores (*Helleborus orientalis*) can stay colorful until the crocuses (*Crocus*) and daffodils (*Narcissus*) appear in the early days of spring.

For all these reasons then, companionable plants grown together make good gardens. With a little care and attention they reward the gardener with long and rich harvests and lovely feasts for the eye.

Here is a good example of flowering plants and vegetables growing together. Such mixtures are not only attractive to look at, but benefit from each other's company as well. Many flowering plants help repel insect pests, while others help attract insects that prey on pests, such as lacewings and hoverflies. Flowers can be planted in separate rows or interplanted in the same rows with the vegetables. Both methods are used here, creating not only a good environment in which the plants can grow, but also one that is pleasant for the gardener to work in.

COMPANION PLANTING–
A COTTAGE GARDEN TRADITION

To discover the beginnings of companion planting one must go back to the cottage gardens, those small, closely planted gardens where vegetables were often mixed with both flowers and herbs.

Cottage gardening evolved slowly in Europe over many centuries. It grew up as a matter of necessity; plants were needed to keep the family alive. Initially gardens, or more likely primitive enclosures near the house, were probably restricted to the growing of herbs for medicinal and culinary purposes; the vegetables were grown in fields that were more like modern smallholdings. As the peasants became stripped of their land they concentrated their vegetable growing into cottage gardens similar to what we think of today when we use that term. In the nineteenth century, many gardens were moved once again outside the confines of land around the house, this time to the allotment or to community garden plots. Here they continued to use techniques they had evolved in the cottage garden and, in many ways, the allotment is still one of the great bastions of cottage gardening, or companion planting, techniques.

The companion planting techniques that were used evolved out of experience. This experience was handed down from generation to generation, any changes being made as new methods were discovered by the cottager himself or shared by friends, possibly often the gardener at the "big house." Many gardening theories of the time were tested at the big house, by its army of gardeners, before they were adopted by the cottager, for his techniques had to be successful or he and his family were likely to go hungry.

While many of the cottages maintained very attractive flower borders, as can be seen in the many watercolors done in the nineteenth century, there was very little time to spend on them. Country people were hard working, and spare time was more likely to be spent on the more productive vegetable gardens. The flower gardens, then, had to be easy to maintain and if possible look after themselves for long periods of the year. So gardeners would choose flowers that got along well together, that more or less helped each other create an environment beneficial to all, and that kept the garden in bloom spring, summer, and fall, with interest provided by bark and berries in the winter.

The cottage garden has great appeal today because we are attracted to its well-intended informality, to its gentle interplay of so many kinds of plants. It has another great attraction, and that is that it creates a more natural environment in which plants can thrive so, once established, there is less maintenance involved.

The cottage garden tradition is still alive today in many country areas, where vegetables and flowers are found growing side by side. The cabbages and dahlias (Dahlia) seen here both like rich, deeply tilled soil and therefore grow well together.

FUTURE IN THE PAST

Although gardeners plant for the future, they do so with a firm eye on the traditions of the past. Tested theories have been handed down from generation to generation. Earlier gardeners learned not only from their own experience but also from that of their families, friends, and from writers. Once printing was firmly established a large number of books, periodicals, and informative seed catalogues became available to those who could read.

The Gardeners Labyrinth.   25

the benefits of walks and Allies in anie Garden-ground: which the Gardener of his owne experience may artly tread out by a line, and sift ouer with sand, if the owner will, for the causes afore vttered.

The forme of the disposing the quarters into beddes, and apt borders about, with the sowing, choise and defence of the seedes, and weeding of the beddes.   Chap.13.

The quarters well turned in, and fatned with good dung a time before, & the earth raised through the dunging, shal in handsome maner by a line set downe in the earth, be troden out into beddes and seemely borders, which beds (as Columella witnesseth) raysed newly afore with dung, and finely raked ouer, with the clods dissolued, and stones

ABOVE *Undoubtedly the most popular reading has always been the seed catalogues, which provide gardeners with a very wide range of tantalizing subjects to grow. More so in the past but to a certain extent still today, gardeners save seed from their own plants but were – and are – always on the lookout for novelties and new disease-resistant strains.*

LEFT *The current interest in dividing the garden into small plots that can be easily reached without having to tread on the soil is not a new idea. Most of today's trends in organic and companion gardening have their base in tradition.*

MIXED CULTURES RATHER THAN MONOCULTURES

One of the lessons that the cottager learned was that it is better to mix crops, be it vegetables or flowers. A lot of different types of crops were likely to provide an overall better harvest, or, in the case of flowers, a better show, than planting larger areas of just a few. Concentration on one crop could spell disaster.

The classic example of this was the total reliance on the potato as the food crop in Ireland in the mid-nineteenth century. Potato blight swept the country for several years running, causing a great famine in which nearly two million people either died or emigrated to avoid its effects.

The same thing can happen in the flower garden. Concentrate all your *Phlox*, for example, in one border and trouble is liable to ensue. If nematodes arrive they will quickly build up into vast numbers and distort and kill the plants, preventing you from reusing that ground for *Phlox* again for several years. On the other hand, *Phlox* spread around the garden, separated by other plants, means the chances are that if one clump is attacked the others will escape harm.

Monocultures are much more prone to disease and pests than mixed plantings, and there is evidence that yields are not as great as when several crops are grown together. Modern farming and horticulture techniques that rely on monocropping, particularly greenhouse culture, depend upon chemicals to keep plants healthy. Intermixing the crops reduces the chances of one disease destroying the whole harvest and increases the opportunity for populations of beneficial insects to prey on pests.

Allotment or community gardens provide an opportunity to practice companion planting on a large scale. Each plot has its own layout with different varieties of vegetables and flowering plants. The mixed environment attracts pests, but it also attracts a large number of predators, helping to keep a healthy balance.

Monocultures, or a concentration of one crop, allow pests or diseases to multiply rapidly once they get hold, resulting in the reliance on pesticides, fungicides, and other chemicals to control the condition. (If indeed control is possible; in some cases, particularly with viral infections, there is still no adequate chemical control.)

A mixed culture has many advantages, most of which will emerge in the pages of this book. One of the main ones is that while there are liable to be more different types of pests in such a garden, there are also going to be more predators. No one pest is likely to build up into unmanageable proportions. For example, even in a bad outbreak of aphids, which seems to like more different host plants than most other insects, it rarely gets out of hand in a truly mixed garden, because there always

seem to be enough ladybugs, lacewings, hoverflies (also known as syrphid flies and flower flies), and other insects which keep the infestation under control.

On the other hand, in a garden devoted to just roses, for example, or a large area assigned to broad beans, the greenfly or blackfly could easily gain the upper hand if insecticide is not used.

Cottagers did not have chemicals readily available; they had to deal with pests in other ways. One way (and we will read about others later) was to mix their plantings. Although this was a practical solution to a real problem, as with so many simple techniques it ended up having other advantages as well; for this reason the cottage garden is probably the most attractive of all gardening styles.

15

CHAPTER ONE

THE GARDEN FRAMEWORK

Before a garden can be established two important tasks must be accomplished: the soil must be prepared carefully and there should be some shelter from extremes of weather. Shelter need not be dull and uninteresting, as the lovely mixed hedge on the left shows.

SOIL PREPARATION

Of all garden tasks, soil preparation is probably the most important. This includes adding vital nutrients and humus, in the form of compost and manures, to the soil to replace that used up the previous year.

USING COMPOSTS

Well-rotted compost adds nutrients and texture to the soil. It can be incorporated as the soil is being dug. Dig out one spade full of earth and place some compost in the trench that has been formed. Dig out the next spade full, placing it on top of the compost. Put more compost in the new trench and continue until the whole plot has been dug.

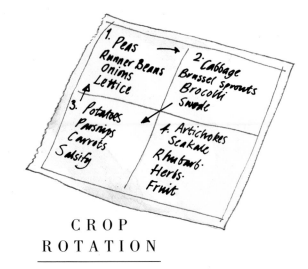

CROP ROTATION

Rotating crops helps to get the best from the soil and keeps down pests and diseases. A rough sketch is essential so that space is provided for all the crops that you want to grow.

GREEN MANURES

By growing green manures you are making use of your garden while it is idle to produce its own fertilizers and soil conditioners. Quick-growing crops such as mustard (above) are sown and then turned into the soil just before sowing or planting the main crop. *Phacelia tanacetifolia* (right) is another green manure.

COVER CROPS

Cover crops are planted in idle gardens to protect them from soil erosion, the worst effects of which can be seen right. Most often they are green manure crops that are turned into the soil just before the gardening season begins again.

BUCKWHEAT

Some crops serve more than one purpose. Buckwheat, for example, is often used as a green manure, but it also attracts garden hoverflies, which feed on aphids and blackflies, and thus helps to keep the populations of these pests under control.

KITCHEN WASTE

Any organic, non-animal waste from the kitchen, particularly peelings and cores, can be used on the compost heap. Even old tea bags can be used. Beware of including animal waste, in particular meat, as this may attract rats and other vermin.

COMPOST

Compost is one of the most valuable garden soil conditioners – and it is free. Any material from the garden that will decompose can be used. The addition of some farmyard manure will help speed up the process and will add to its value. If possible have more than one bin, as it is a good idea to be adding material to one while taking the finished compost from the other.

CLEANING AND PREPARING THE GROUND

When faced with a new or neglected piece of ground, there is a strong temptation to go at it as fast as one can to get it planted and in production. This can spell disaster since the ground is bound to be full of weeds. Time spent during the first season cleaning and thoroughly preparing the soil will certainly bear dividends in the long term. Although this is true for both vegetable and flower borders, it is the flower borders that need particular attention, since once planted you may not want to disturb them for many years. Vegetables are dug over every year, giving you opportunities to discover and dig out weeds missed earlier.

There is no better way of preparing the ground than by hand digging it over and then hand weeding to remove all the perennial weeds as you go.

Once the ground has been dug it can be left fallow to allow annual weeds to germinate. These can be hoed off at regular intervals. However, many gardeners would find that leaving the ground fallow is a waste of a valuable natural resource. There are certain crops which are ideal to grow in weedy ground that has recently been dug up. Potatoes and brassicas (vegetables in the cabbage family), are two such crops that are regularly used by gardeners in such situations.

They both have advantages above and below ground. Below ground, the extensive and, in the case of the cabbages, deep and strong roots help break up the new ground. The deeper rooted they are, the better. Another advantage with cabbages is that it is easy to hoe right up to the plants, something which it is difficult to do with, for example, a row of carrots. Any weeds can be removed and the ground kept in good condition, encouraging other weed seeds to grow so that by the end of the season the number of seeds waiting to germinate in the soil has been drastically diminished. Growing potatoes is beneficial in a similar way, except here the soil is kept disturbed as the rows are earthed up. The large amount of foliage also helps kill off struggling weeds.

As mentioned in the section on green manuring, there are other plants with strong tap roots which help to break up the lower levels of the soil and bring nutrients up to the surface where they can be more readily used by the next season's crops.

To double dig, cut a trench across the width of the plot, putting the soil to one side (1). Loosen the bottom of the trench with a fork and place compost or farmyard manure on top (2). Then fill the trench with soil dug from the next trench (3). Continue this process down the plot, using the surplus soil from the first row to fill the final trench.

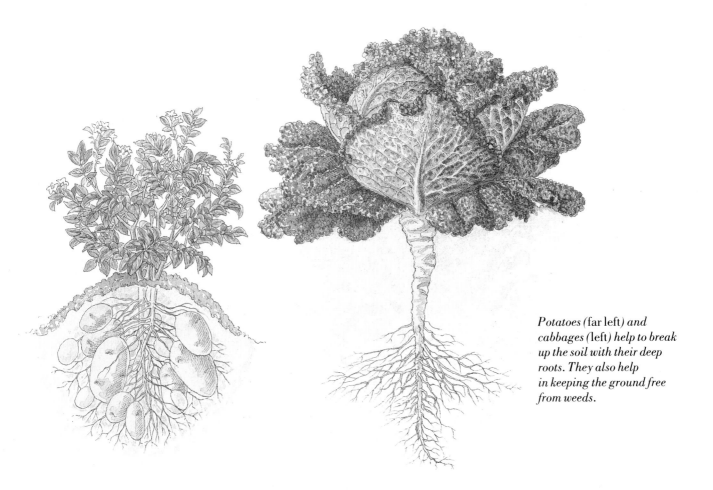

Potatoes (far left) and cabbages (left) help to break up the soil with their deep roots. They also help in keeping the ground free from weeds.

LEFT *A dark, free-draining but moisture-retentive soil is what every gardener longs for. Annual digging with plenty of humus and the use of deep-rooted plants will help to achieve this. Even a heavy soil can eventually be turned into one with a light, friable texture.*

SOIL ENRICHMENT

Soil can be enriched and conditioned in a number of ways. In the garden, doing it organically, with the use of live material (green manuring) and dead material (compost, manure), is safer to human health and in many cases less expensive than using inorganic, or chemical, fertilizers.

Using certain crops as green manure has been practiced for generations. It involves growing a crop on idle land and then digging it into the ground rather than harvesting it. Tilling or digging in the plant material adds both organic material (for better texture) and nutrients (for improved fertility) to the soil, thereby cutting down or eliminating entirely the need for chemical fertilizers.

When the green manure is dug into the ground it rots, as it would in a compost heap, leaving a certain amount of humus in the soil which is vital for the soil's texture, or structure. It also leaves behind a residue of nutrients that it produced while growing. In the case of deep-rooted plants, important elements in the soil are brought up from deep down in the soil and made available to shallow-rooted crops that are planted to follow the green manure. Leguminous plants (peas and lupins, for example) can do some of the work of nitrogen fertilizers. They will actually take nitrogen, an element essential for plant growth, from the air and "fix" it in the soil, making it then available to plants.

Another advantage of green manures is that they act as cover crops. In many areas soil that is left bare between the harvesting of one crop and the sowing of the next is prone to erosion by wind or water run-off. The planting of a fast-growing, intermediate crop helps prevent this. It also helps keep the plot free from weeds.

To be most effective, the seed of the cover crop is sown as soon as possible after the main crop has been harvested. The soil may need digging or it may be sufficient just to rake it over, depending on its condition. The seed can be scattered or sown in drills. Shortly before the next crop is due to be sown, the green manure is chopped off, left to wilt, and then dug into the soil. The cover crop should not be allowed to get to the stage where it is likely to flower. If it does flower and then go to seed there will be a repeat crop, setting up competition to the main crop planted next.

Some green manures, such as mustard, are very fast growing and can be used on pieces of ground that are empty for only a few weeks. The deeper-rooted crops, legumes for instance, are best left in the ground for much longer periods of time, up to a year, to get their full benefit.

*Lupins (*Lupinus angustifolius*) are widely used for soil enrichment. As well as supplying nitrogen to the soil, their deep roots are good at breaking up the deeper levels and providing a fine tilth. They can be planted in a block and dug into the soil as the flower buds are formed, or a few plants can be planted around the garden and allowed to flower before they are dug in.*

TYPES OF GREEN MANURE

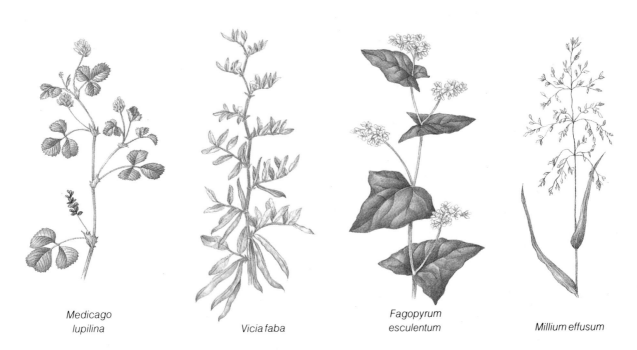

Medicago lupilina

Vicia faba

Fagopyrum esculentum

Millium effusum

NITROGEN FIXERS

Alfalfa (*Medicago sativa*). Also known as lucerne. Very deep-rooted plant. Valuable for adding nitrogen. Helps condition the subsoil. Sow in spring or fall. Dig in during the following fall or spring.

Alsike clover (*Trifolium hybridum*). Good for nitrogen. A good clover for heavy or wet soils. Sow in spring or early fall. Dig in when required.

Black medic (*Medicago lupilina*). Also known as hop clover. Nitrogen fixer related to alfalfa. Sow in spring or fall. Dig in as required.

Cowpea (*Vigna unguiculata*). Nitrogen fixer also useful for breaking up hard-packed soil with its powerful roots. Crop can be allowed to seed and can then be eaten. Sow in spring. Harvest and dig in vines when ready.

Fava beans (*Vicia faba*). Also known as broad beans. Supplies nitrogen and quantities of green manure. Can be left to seed so that crop can be harvested and eaten. Sow in spring or fall, dig in any time up to and including seeding time.

Lupins (*Lupinus angustifolius*). Deep-rooting plant that adds nitrogen and phosphates to the soil. Sow in spring and dig in just as the flower buds form. Another crop can be sown in fall.

Red clover (*Trifolium pratense*). Good nitrogen fixer with good amount of top growth for green manure. Sow in spring. Dig in well in fall.

Winter tare (*Vicia villosa*). Good nitrogen fixer and weed suppressor for the winter months. Sow in fall, dig in the following spring.

NON-NITROGEN FIXERS

Annual ryegrass (*Lolium multiflorum*). Fast growing with good amount of top growth. Sow in early spring, dig in before flowering.

Buckwheat (*Fagopyrum esculentum*). Good for acid soils. Extensive and vigorous root system. Tall with lots of good top growth. Sow in early summer. Dig in during fall.

Attracts hoverflies which are predators of aphids.

Comfrey (*Symphytum* × *uplandicum*). Unlike the others which are grown right in the beds, this is grown as a separate perennial crop. The leaves, full of nitrogen and minerals, are harvested and dug into the vegetable beds.

Millet (*Millium effusum*). A good green manure plant for dry or poor soils. Sow in spring, dig in before flowering.

Mustard (*Sinapsis alba*). Most popular garden green manure. Very quick growing with good amount of top growth. Good weed suppressant. Sow any time and dig in at any stage before flowering.

Phacelia (*Phacelia tanacetifolia*). Fast growing with good-quality top growth. Sow late in spring and dig in from summer onward.

Rye (*Ecale cereale*). Extensive roots and good top growth. Sow in fall and dig in during spring.

COMPOSTS

Of all the material that can be added to the soil, including chemicals, the most valuable is properly decayed organic matter, or compost. It not only adds valuable nutrients, it also provides fibrous humus which helps to improve the soil's texture, or structure. It helps to break down the heavier soils, at the same time providing lighter soils with a medium that will retain moisture. It holds just enough for the plants' needs without causing them to be surrounded by stagnant water, a condition few plants will tolerate.

Compost can be made from crops deliberately grown for that purpose, comfrey (*Symphytum × uplandicum*) being a very good example, or from waste organic material from the garden. It is surprising how much vegetable and fruit waste can come from the kitchen.

At its simplest the compost heap is just a pile of weeds, lawn cuttings, and soft prunings, with perhaps some farmyard manure added. This heap will warm up, providing the nice warm and moist environment that will encourage bacteria to get to work, breaking it down into a crumbly consistency.

A compost container can make this process happen more efficiently. The container will not only keep all the material neat, it will also help to maintain its temperature and prevent too much rain from penetrating the layers. A compost bin can be made of any material as long as there are holes to allow air to penetrate and a lid to keep the heat in and the rain out, an old carpet or sheet of plastic can be suitable for this.

The composting material is best added to the heap in layers: a layer of grass cuttings followed by a layer of vegetable waste, followed in turn by weeds and so on, each layer being about 6in (15cm) thick. Any material, such as grass cuttings, that could mat together and make a solid lump, preventing the circulation of air, should be mixed with another material to lighten it. Bacteria, which is a vital part in the making of the compost, needs nitrogen as a "starter" to get the process going. Farmyard manure is the ideal nitrogen material, but special compost activators can be bought if manure is not available. If there is not much soil on the weeds, a covering of good topsoil between every four or five layers is beneficial. A sprinkling of lime should be added every

Ideal compost bins, made from planks of wood. The newly added material can be seen through the gaps at the top and the ready compost through those at the bottom (right). It's best to have two bins (above) so that one can be filled while the other is being emptied.

few layers to keep the heap from becoming too acid. A compost heap needs water, and in a dry season a few buckets of water might be added.

Weeds that are in seed should not be added to the heap, as the compost rarely gets hot enough to kill them off. Avoid using any disease-infested material or anything, cabbage stalks for instance, that is too thick or woody to break down.

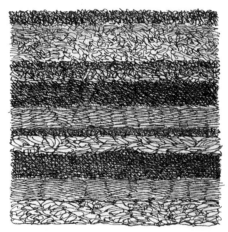

layer of topsoil

weeds

kitchen waste
fine lime
farmyard manure

grass cuttings
layer of topsoil
crop residue
farmyard manure
fine lime

grass cuttings

soft hedge trimmings

ABOVE *Composted material should be added in layers.*

BELOW *Bins can be made of any material, including honeycombed brickwork, wire mesh, or corrugated iron; the latter is fine so long as there are sufficient holes to allow air to get in.*

ALTERNATIVES TO COMPOSTS

Different composts possess different qualities. Some have a high nutritional value, while others are negligible in terms of the goodness they put into the soil.

Composted bark This has become more readily available in recent years. Contains little nutrient value but is high in humus. Particularly good as a mulch.

Chicken manure Very strong manure that should be stored for several months before use. Useful for adding as an activator in a compost heap.

Farmyard manure Well-rotted farmyard manure, containing dung from cattle, horses, sheep, or pigs, is excellent for conditioning soil. Contains a high level of nutrients and the straw provides plenty of humus. Often contains weed seed, so doubtful as a mulch.

Leafmold Slower to decompose than normal garden compost, but valuable both for its nutrients and humus. Very good as a mulch.

Peat No nutritional value. Useful in adding humus to the soil or as a mulch, but breaks down quickly.

Seaweed A very good soil conditioner containing nutrients including valuable trace elements. Best dug into the soil, but can be used as a mulch.

Spent hops Left over from the beer-making process it contains only a little nutrient value, but is useful for adding humus to the soil or as a mulch.

Spent mushroom compost Various mixtures used in growing mushrooms, usually including farmyard manure. Good value in both nutrients and bulk. Good for conditioning soil or as a mulch. It also includes chalk so do not use on plants that dislike lime.

PROTECTING THE GARDEN

Plants need protecting from adverse weather, particularly strong winds. Hedges are the most attractive way of providing shelter.

PROVIDING A BACKDROP

A hedge not only provides necessary protection against winds and farm animals, it also makes a background against which flowering plants can be seen with advantage. Here a colorful border is shown off against a dark green yew hedge.

PLANTING A HEDGE

A strip 4ft (1.2m) wide along the line of the hedge must be thoroughly prepared, preferably double-dug and incorporating plenty of organic material. Planting should be at any time between late fall and spring when weather allows. Distances between plants vary according to type but are generally in the region of 1-2ft (30-60cm). Prune back by a half after planting. Protect with a temporary plastic or **gunnysack** screen in windy areas and do not allow the young plants to dry out.

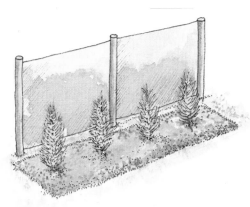

well-shaped hedge   well-shaped hedge   well-shaped hedge   badly shaped hedge

MAINTENANCE OF HEDGES

The frequency of cutting hedges varies according to the speed of growth. Informal hedges usually only require cutting once a year, immediately after flowering. The width of the hedge should be narrower at the top. This helps with stability and prevents damage by snow. Treat hedges as ordinary shrubs, feeding them annually with farmyard manure or compost and ensuring that they do not get too dry.

SILVER-LEAVED PLANTS

Artemisia stelleriana (above) silver-leaved plants are generally sun lovers, and should be planted where they are not shaded by other plants.

VARIEGATED PLANTS

Variegated plants, such as *Ilex × altaclerensis* 'Silver Sentinel' shown right, often burn in hot midday sun and should be sheltered by other plants.

PLANTS PROTECTING PLANTS AGAINST THE ELEMENTS

One of the greatest challenges in gardening is the constant battle with the elements. In some places it is a question of modifying the existing climate by sheltering plants from the wind, providing shade or moisture; in others it is anticipating sudden swings from one temperature extreme to another. In one part of the country or another, there seems to be a constant stream of the "coldest winter," "driest summer," or the "strongest wind," all of which put plants under severe stress.

Few gardeners are lucky enough to garden in ideal conditions; the majority have to modify their gardens in an attempt to remove the worst extremes. In many cases this is possible by bringing in other plants to help.

One of plants' enemies is the wind. It can do damage by breaking them with its force, or by causing wind-burn to the leaves. It can also cause indirect damage by drying out the soil, thus denying plants moisture, or by eroding the soil around them. Windbreaks – man-made structures or tall plantings that break the force of the wind – are the answer.

Wood fences, walls of brick and stone, or screens of plastic netting can all protect plants from wind. A barrier will protect plants standing on the leeward side

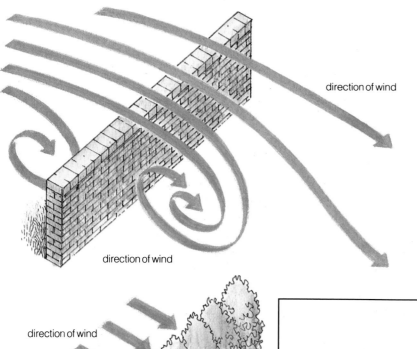

direction of wind

direction of wind

direction of wind

LEFT *Solid barriers, such as walls, make poor windbreaks because they create a turbulence, which is as destructive as the wind itself. Barriers that allow the wind to filter through reduce the wind speed dramatically but do not create the turbulence. Hedges, plastic netting, or slatted fences all make good windbreaks, but hedges are preferable in a companionable garden.*

BELOW *The wind speed will be reduced over a horizontal distance equivalent to thirty times the height of the screen, but the most significant and useful drop is over the first third of this – up to ten times the height.*

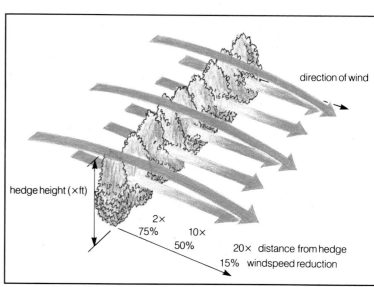

direction of wind

hedge height (×ft)

2×
75%   10×
50%
20× distance from hedge
15% windspeed reduction

for a distance up to ten times the height of the barrier. However, if this is solid, such as a wall, severe turbulence will be created. Open fences and plastic netting are much more effective, as they allow the wind to filter through, giving the required protection on the leeward side.

While fences and netting have their place, hedges are by far the most attractive option. They may need cutting and the leaves may need clearing up, but they usually make a much more sympathetic background to a garden. Hedges have the qualities of a good windbreak: they allow the wind to filter through and have a certain amount of flexibility in high gusts. They are also "adjustable," as they can be allowed to grow a little taller or be cut back until the best effect is achieved.

Hedges can be grown from a wide range of shrubs or trees, but it is best to avoid vigorous-growing ones. Although these will quickly get to the required height, they will not stop growing, and they will need much more subsequent attention than a slower-growing choice.

Frost is another hazard in many gardens. Tender plants can be grown up against a wall that faces the winter sun or near trees and shrubs in similar positions. Some plants need covering in winter to give them added

TAPESTRY HEDGES

A hedge need not be all of the same material. Cottage garden hedges often were, and still are, a mixture of all kinds of shrubs. Mine consist of beech (*Fagus*), holly (*Ilex*), hawthorn (*Crataegus*), hazel (*Corylus avellana*), privet (*Ligustrum*), trailing honeysuckle (*Lonicera*), blackberries (*Rubus*), oak (*Quercus*), snowberry (*Symphoricarpos*), box (*Buxus*), lilac, *Lonicera nitida*, and a few other odds and ends. This makes a wonderful tapestry of different colors and textures. The big problem is that all these plants grow at different rates, hence it can look a bit ragged. In the country this does not matter, but in town it can look out of place and must be cut regularly to keep it neat and tidy.

A more conventional tapestry hedge that needs much less attention can be created by choosing different clones of the same species. For example using alternate ordinary green and copper beeches (*Fagus sylvestris*) can form an attractive hedge. Similarly alternate green privet (*Ligustrum ovalifolium*) and golden privet (*L. o.* 'Variegatum') can be used. If flowering shrubs are used, choosing those that have complementary colored flowers could provide lovely contrast. For example, white and red rugosa roses (*Rosa rugosa*) make an attractive informal hedge.

BELOW LEFT *Box elder (*Acer negundo *'Variegata') and* Prunus cerasifera *make a classic bicolored hedge.*
BELOW RIGHT *A convent-* *ional hedge for most of the year, the azaleas* (Rhododendron) *provide a tapestry when they are in flower.*

protection, and here dead plant materials such as bracken or straw make a warm mulch.

Frost will often roll down slopes, even quite small slopes, and accumulate in frost hollows at the bottom. These hollows can often be created on the side of a hill when frost, rolling down the slope, is stopped by a hedgerow. A pool of cold air forms on the upward side of the hedge, causing a pocket of frost. This air can be drained away by leaving gaps in the hedge at its lowest point. By this means the temperature of a garden can be increased by several degrees. Similarly, cold air can be diverted by the inclusion of hedges along the upper edge of the garden. These should be angled in such a way as to send any descending cold air around the garden.

Hot sunshine is another problem for many plants. Some, which prefer shade, can be kept happy in the open by keeping them moist and never letting them dry out, but the easiest way is to provide some sort of shade. Here trees and shrubs can be utilized. It is best to avoid those with shallow roots – ash (*Fraxinus*) or birch (*Betula*) for example – or those that cast too much shade – like beech (*Fagus*) or yew (*Taxus*) – as these create difficult conditions in which to establish other plants. A light, dappled shade is best. Unless the sun is directly overhead at some point in the day, it is often sufficient to place the plants alongside a shrub rather than under it.

Not much can be done with plants to alleviate the shortage of water, but they can still be a help by the way of indicators. In areas where there is rain throughout the year but at irregular intervals, possibly with drying sun or winds in between, it often happens that gardeners lose track of what moisture there is in the soil; it can be much drier than they realize. One way to solve this problem is

Cold air moving down a slope will gather against a solid hedge or fence to form a frost pocket several degrees colder than the surrounding air. If the hedge is pierced by a gate or by gaps, then the cold air will drain away. Similarly, if a curved or "v"-shaped hedge is planted at the top of the slope it will divert the frosty air around the garden.

to plant some drought indicators: plants that show at an early stage that the soil is beginning to dry out and that it is time to start applying water artificially. *Hydrangea*, *Astilbe*, and *Veronica longifolia* are all plants whose leaves will start drooping as soon as moisture becomes scarce. If you apply water as soon as this is seen, no losses should occur in the borders because of drought.

Drainage is a problem that must be dealt with when the garden is laid out; it is not a problem that can be solved with plants. Few plants will tolerate excess water and a few detest virtually any moisture during the winter when they are in their dormant stage. A sheet of glass or other screen placed over the latter is one solution, but there are some plants such as *Cistus* that benefit from being planted close under trees which will remove excess water from the soil for their own needs.

ABOVE *Mulching plants helps protect them against excessive loss of moisture from the soil and against competing weeds. It also helps prevent the roots from freezing in a cold winter. Here straw can be seen around the base of a shrub.*

ABOVE *This fig tree is protected by a bracken screen. The best way to cope with frost is only to grow hardy plants, but it is tempting to try something a bit more tender once in a while. Plastic netting provides protection, as does bracken, which is a more natural and effective covering that adds a warm glow to the winter scene. Straw or evergreen branches can also be used.*

PHYSICAL BARRIERS

Plants can give protection to one another in ways other than against the weather; they can provide physical protection, particularly against animals. After all, hedges were first used to keep livestock either in or out of a field or garden.

One of the most effective animalproof hedges is of quickthorn, or hawthorn, (*Crataegus monogyna*). This forms a dense prickly hedge that does not need too much attention, only one or two cuts a year depending on how neat you like your hedges to look. Holly (*Ilex aquifolium*) has similar qualities except that it is evergreen. Various *Berberis* species provide a good hedge, but if these are to flower then they cannot be cut too regularly, resulting in a bit of sprawling. Any prickly hedge has one severe disadvantage to the gardener: if there are any borders near the hedge which need regular weeding it is inevitable that some of the prickly leaves or thorns will find their way into the fingers or under the fingernails of the weeder.

Animalproof hedges do not have to be prickly, as long as they are dense right to the ground; this is sufficient to keep most farm animals out. Deer are a bit of a problem, as these can jump over quite high obstacles, so any hedge grown to keep them at bay must be at least 8ft (2.5m) high. It must be dense, otherwise they can push their way through.

Hedges are no deterrent to animals such as rabbits. One way of keeping rabbits out is first to put up a galvanized wire fence, burying 6-10in (15-25cm) in the ground. Then plant the hedge next to this so that it grows through it. The fence is soon obscured from view but will remain effective as long as the galvanizing prevents it from rusting.

Prickly plants can be used elsewhere in the garden to deter domestic animals, for example, from being too much of a nuisance. If cats insist on climbing in a delicate shrub or plant, a few branches of *Berberis* will keep them at a distance.

Another benefit of a hedge should be mentioned, although it is more to protect people than plants. A good thick hedge gives the gardener privacy and does, to a certain extent, absorb noise. If you like peace and quiet in your garden, this could be a real advantage.

ABOVE *To keep out rabbits put up a galvanized wire fence burying 6-10in (15-25cm) in the ground. Plant a hedge next to it.*

LEFT *Holly (*Ilex aquifolium*) makes an ideal hedge. It is evergreen, animalproof, and only needs cutting once or twice a year. The only disadvantage is that the sharp-edged fallen leaves make it painful to weed any beds in the vicinity.*

PLANTS FOR ANIMALPROOF HEDGES

Below are a selection of the very best plants to choose for animalproof hedges. They all have the advantage of creating dense, thick barriers over a period of time.

DECIDUOUS	
Plant name	**Characteristics**
Beech *Fagus sylvatica*	slow growing, keeps leaves in winter
Blackthorn *Prunus spinosa*	quick growing, viscious spines
Field maple *Acer campestre*	best in mixed hedge
Hawthorn, or quick thorn *Crataegus monogyna*	quick growing, spiny
Hornbeam *Carpinus betulus*	slow growing, keeps leaves in winter
Roses *Rosa rugosa*	spiny, decorative flowers and hips, informal
Sea buckthorn *Hippophae rhamnoides*	spiny, informal

EVERGREEN	
Berberis *Berberis × stenophylla*	spiny, decorative flowers, informal
Escallonia *Escallonia*	informal, decorative flowers
Holly *Ilex aquifolium*	spiny
Leyland cypress *× Cupressocyparis leylandii*	quick growing
Privet *Ligustrum ovalifolium*	quick growing
Yew *Taxus baccata*	poisonous to some animals, slow growing

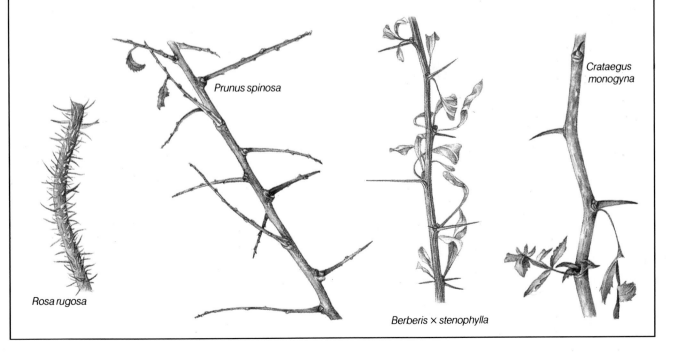

Prunus spinosa

Crataegus monogyna

Rosa rugosa

Berberis × stenophylla

CHAPTER TWO

FRUIT, VEGETABLES, & HERBS

Perhaps we will not starve without our gardens, but by growing our own fruit and vegetables we are able to have almost any varieties we want and with much better flavor than that of bought produce. We also know that no chemicals have been used. On a less practical level, a well-stocked vegetable garden (*left*) is a satisfying sight.

GOOD GARDENING TECHNIQUES

Sowing seed is one of the fundamental techniques of gardening. Choosing the right seed and getting it off to a good start can make all the difference to the final harvest.

SEED LISTS

Most vegetables are grown from seed. This can be either purchased from seed companies or kept from one's own plants. Lavish seed lists are produced which list many varieties of each vegetable. There is no rule of thumb as to which of these will grow well in your own area. Talk to other gardeners and find out which particular varieties do well for them: which do they find to be the most disease-resistant, the most tasty, and the most prolific. Experiment with different varieties until you find those that suit you and your ground best. Once you have found these stick to them, but perhaps grow a few experimental rows each year of untried varieties.

STORAGE LIFE OF SEEDS

Seed unused one year can be saved to the next, but the length of its viability varies. The fresher the seed, the greater will be the germination rate. Below is a table of the maximum amount of time vegetable seed can be kept after the packet has been opened.

Vegetable	Useful life of seed
Beet	4 years
Borecole	4 years
Broad bean	1 year
Broccoli	4 years
Brussels sprout	4 years
Cabbage	4 years
Carrot	3 years
Cauliflower	4 years
Celeriac	5 years
Celery	5 years
Chinese cabbage	4 years
Cucumber	6 years
French bean	1 year
Kale	4 years
Kohlrabi	4 years
Leek	3 years
Lettuce	3 years
Onion	3 years
Parsley	1 year
Parsnip	use straight away
Pea	1 year
Purple sprouting	4 years
Radish	3 years
Runner bean	1 year
Rutabaga	1 year
Salsify	1 year
Scorzonera	use straight away
Spinach	1 year
Spinach-beet	4 years
Summer squash	6 years
Turnips	1 year
Zucchini	6 years

GERMINATION RATES

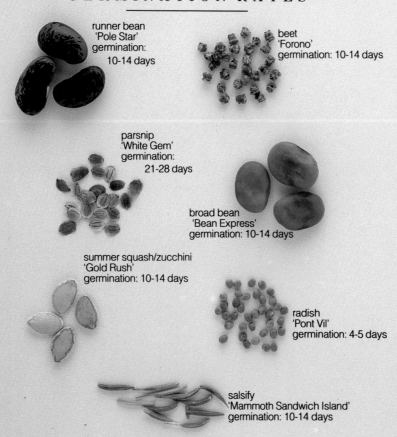

runner bean 'Pole Star' germination: 10-14 days

beet 'Forono' germination: 10-14 days

parsnip 'White Gem' germination: 21-28 days

broad bean 'Bean Express' germination: 10-14 days

summer squash/zucchini 'Gold Rush' germination: 10-14 days

radish 'Pont Vil' germination: 4-5 days

salsify 'Mammoth Sandwich Island' germination: 10-14 days

SOWING POTATOES

Potatoes are prepared for sowing by placing them in a single
layer on a tray or shallow box in a light, but frost-free shed.
When short shoots appear, they are ready for sowing. A trench
is dug in well-prepared soil and the seed potatoes are laid out
along the trench at 12in (30cm) intervals. The earth is raked
over the potatoes and then heaped up, forming a ridge along the
length of the row. As the shoots of the young potatoes appear,
the ridge is made larger until it is about 12in (30cm) high.
A healthy-looking crop of potatoes can be seen in the
photograph below.

STORING VEGETABLES

Some crops such as leeks, parsnips, and rutabagas will
overwinter in the ground. Many other root crops, such as
carrots and beets, need digging up and storing under frost-free
conditions.

The vegetables should be dug up on a dry day. Allow the soil
to dry on the roots and then rub it off. Cut through the leaf stems
just above the top of the root. Store them in boxes of dry peat
moss or sand, keeping each individual separate from its
neighbor. Store only sound produce. Any blemished
vegetables should be cooked first as these
will rot if stored. In areas prone to long
periods of frost all root crops can be
stored in this way.

SOWING LARGE SEEDS

Plants with large seeds such as summer squash,
cucumbers, pumpkins, and beans can be sown
individually in pots. This obviates the need for
thinning out and reduces the amount of set back
that this produces. It also makes it easier to
plant them out.

SOWING AND PLANTING

Seed can be sown directly into the ground or in pots and trays. Basically the technique is the same in both cases: provide a moist, warm habitat in which the seed can germinate. It should be as free from competition as possible.

In the open garden the soil should be dug over, digging in the green manure crop if you planted one, and raking it into a fine tilth. If the intention is to sow in rows, then draw out a shallow drill, about ½in (1.25cm) deep for most seed, but as deep as 2in (5cm) for large seed such as beans and peas. The drill can be kept straight by the use of a string line stretched between two sticks as a guide. The distance between the rows will depend on the height and spread of the plants.

If the soil is heavy and cannot be broken down into a fine tilth, or if it is very quick draining, a layer of compost from the compost heap can be put into a slightly deeper drill. This will help the germinating seed find a

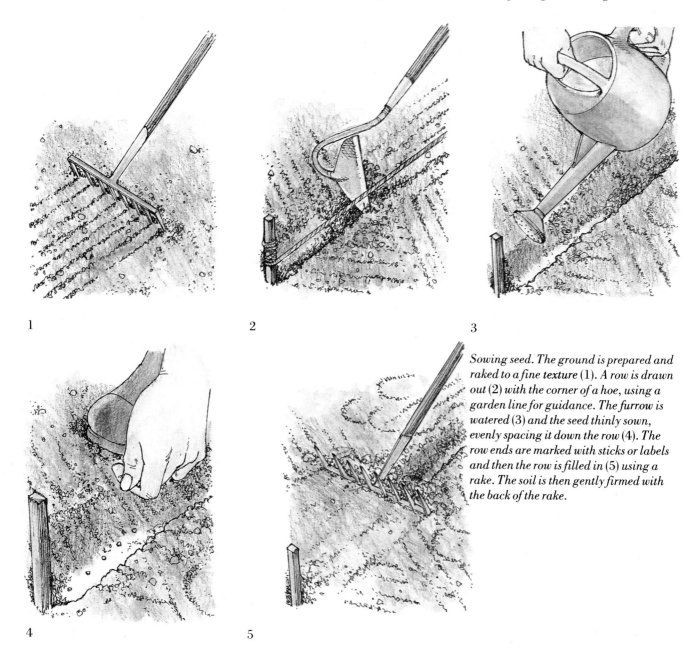

1

2

3

4

5

Sowing seed. The ground is prepared and raked to a fine texture (1). A row is drawn out (2) with the corner of a hoe, using a garden line for guidance. The furrow is watered (3) and the seed thinly sown, evenly spacing it down the row (4). The row ends are marked with sticks or labels and then the row is filled in (5) using a rake. The soil is then gently firmed with the back of the rake.

roothold and keep it moist at this critical stage in its development.

The drill should be watered and the seed thinly sown. With plants that will need quite a bit of space when they mature, like parsnips, they can be station sown. This means sowing three or four seeds at 6-9in (15-23cm) intervals along the drill (larger intervals should be left for larger-growing varieties). Sowing thus saves time thinning out all the intermediate ones at a later stage.

The seed should then be covered with a thin layer of soil and gently firmed down. Each row should be marked and labeled. Labeling may not be very important, but it is surprising how easy it is to forget the name of the variety by the time harvesting comes around. Knowing the variety grown can be important when deciding whether to grow the same one for the following season.

If planting in blocks, the seed can be sown in short rows and then thinned out to give a random pattern, or the seed can be broadcast over the whole area. The soil should have a fine tilth. The seed should be evenly scattered and then raked well into the top ½in (1.25cm) of the soil.

Tray- or pot-sown seed is sown in a fine compost made up of equal parts of loam, sharp sand, and leafmold. The seed is sown on the top and then is covered with a thin layer of the compost. The compost should not be allowed to dry out nor be kept wringing wet.

The majority of seed-sown vegetables are sown in their rows and then left to grow there. The seedlings are thinned out, allowing the strongest to remain at intervals determined by the size of the variety and how big you want them to grow. Parsnips, for example, will grow big if given the space but much smaller if left crammed together, in competition with one another.

After thinning the row should be watered to firm in any soil that was loosened around the remaining seedlings. Evening time, when the sun is not too hot, is a good time to thin.

Thinning carrots can be troublesome, not only because the shoots are so fine and difficult to separate, but also because it can encourage the carrot root fly. This insect can pick up the scent of the carrot plants when the foliage is bruised during thinning. Onions planted nearby help to mask the smell of the carrots, but on still evenings the onion scent will not spread too far. It is better to sow carrot seed as thinly as possible so very little thinning will be needed.

Some plants, such as cabbages, need transplanting after the seeds have grown into seedlings. Keep them well watered before digging them up and, once dug up, replant them as quickly as possible so that they are kept out of the ground for as short a time as possible. Cabbages, in particular, need a firm planting and the ground around the plant should be firmly tamped down

Planting leeks. In order to get good, long, blanched stems, leeks are planted in a trench and then gradually earthed up. A trench 2-3in (5-7.5cm) is dug out and the leeks planted at 6in (15cm) intervals (wider if larger or exhibition leeks are desired). The young leek plants are set into holes which are then filled with water. As the leeks grow the trench is filled in and the earth drawn up around the plants (left). To make the most of space, leeks can be interplanted with lettuce (far left).

SOWING TECHNIQUES

The following table gives details on sowing and planting vegetables. Companion planting (CP) distances are given, as are conventional ones; these may vary according to variety. Seed can be sown in blocks. The resulting plants should be thinned to the recommended intervals, ignoring the suggested distance between rows.

Vegetable	Depth of sowing	Distance apart	Distance between rows	Sowing season	Harvesting season
Beet	¾in (2cm)	8-10in (20-25cm) 4-6in (10-15cm) (CP)	12in (30cm) 8in (20cm) (CP)	mid-spring/ early summer	summer/fall
Broad bean	2in (5cm)	6in (15cm) 4in (10cm) (CP)	24in (60cm)	late fall/ early spring	spring/summer
Brussels sprout	½in (1.25cm)	30in (76cm)	30in (76cm)	spring	fall/winter
Cabbage	½in (1.25cm)	18in (45cm)	18in (45cm)	early spring	summer
Cabbage	½in (1.25cm)	18in (45cm)	18in (45cm)	spring	late fall
Carrot	½in (1.25cm)	4in (10cm) 2in (5cm) (CP)	12in (30cm)	early spring/ early summer	summer onward
Cauliflower	½in (1.25cm)	24in (60cm)	24in (60cm)	spring	fall
Celery	½in (1.25cm)	8in (20cm)	36in (90cm) 24in (60cm) (CP)	spring	fall
Cucumber	¾in (2cm)	24in (60cm)	24in (60cm)	late spring	late summer onward
Dwarf bean	2in (5cm)	6in (15cm) 4in (10cm) (CP)	18in (45cm)	late spring/ early summer	summer/fall
Kohlrabi	½in (1.25cm)	6in (15cm) 4in (10cm) (CP)	12in (30cm) 8in (20cm) (CP)	spring/early summer	summer onward
Leek	½in (1.25cm)	9in (23cm) 6in (15cm) (CP)	12in (30cm) 10in (25cm) (CP)	spring	fall onward

before and after planting. Then water them in well.

A few plants, celery and leeks for example, should be planted in shallow trenches which are gradually filled in and then earthed up around the plants. This process, known as blanching, keeps earth around the stems so that they are not exposed to sunlight, resulting in a tender vegetable.

Plants raised in pots or trays need a bit more attention. They are usually ready for transplanting when the first two true leaves appear (the very first two leaves are the "seed leaves"). Transplanting involves gently removing the plant from potting soil and transferring it to an individual pot or into a larger tray. In either case the procedure is the same. The seedling can be eased out of its soil with a kitchen fork or similar implement. It should be held by its leaves, never the stem or roots which can become fatally damaged in the process. A hole is made in the soil in the pot or tray and the seedling is lowered into it. Once in place the soil around it should be gently packed down so that the seedling is firmed in.

Seeds that have been germinated under glass or indoors in a heated space must be hardened off by allowing them increasing lengths of time in the open air. After about a week of this they are safe to leave outside in their pots or flats. When large enough they can be planted out in the same way as row-grown seedlings.

Vegetable	Depth of sowing	Distance apart	Distance between rows	Sowing season	Harvesting season
Lettuce	½in (1.25cm)	9-12in (23-30cm) 8in (20cm) (CP)	12in (30cm) 10in (25cm) (CP)	spring	spring/ early summer
Onion, sets	1in (2.5cm)	4-6in (10-15cm)	10in (25cm) 8in (20cm) (CP)	spring	late summer
Onion, spring	¼in (0.6cm)	thin as required	6in (15cm)	early spring onward	late spring
Parsnip	½in (1.25cm)	9in (23cm) 6in (15cm) (CP)	12in (30cm)	early spring	fall/winter
Pea	2in (5cm)	2in (5cm)	24-48in (60-120cm)	early spring	early summer
Potato	5in (12.5cm)	15in (38cm)	24in (60cm)	early spring	summer onward
Radish	½in (1.25cm)	thin as required	9in (23cm) 6in (15cm) (CP)	early spring onward	spring onward
Runner bean	2in (5cm)	6in (15cm)	5ft (150cm)	spring	late summer
Salsify	½in (1.25cm)	10in (25cm) 6in (15cm) (CP)	12in (30cm) 10in (25cm) (CP)	late spring	fall
Scorzonera	½in (1.25cm)	10in (25cm) 6in (15cm) (CP)	12in (30cm) 10in (25cm) (CP)	late spring	fall
Shallot, bulbs	1in (2.5cm)	9in (23cm)	9in (23cm)	early spring	summer onward
Spinach	½in (1.25cm)	6in (15cm)	12in (30cm) 10in (25cm) (CP)	early spring	late spring
Summer squash	1in (2.5cm)	24-36in (60-90cm)	24-36in (60-90cm)	spring	summer/fall
Tomato	¼in (0.6cm)	18-24in (45-60cm)	24in (60cm)	late spring	summer/fall
Turnip	½in (1.25cm)	10in (25cm) 6in (15cm) (CP)	12in (30cm) 10in (25cm) (CP)	early spring onward	late spring onward

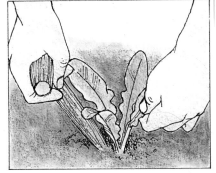

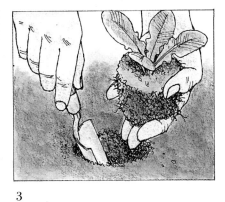

1   2   3

Transplanting and planting out. Seedlings are transplanted into trays, handling them carefully by the leaves (1). Cabbage plants (2) can be placed directly into the soil using a dibble to make the holes and then using it to firm the soil around the plants. Pot-grown plants can be planted with a trowel (3).

41

LAYING OUT CROPS

There are many ways of laying out the crops, depending on what is intended to be grown and the way the plants relate to each other. The visual element should not be forgotten, as it should be a pleasure to work, or just to be, in a garden.

FRUIT

Fruit can be mixed in with vegetables to take advantage of their companionship as a protection against pests. Or it can be kept in a separate area, which makes it easy to construct a fruit cage for keeping out bird and animal pests. The cage should only be kept over the plants while they are in fruit. If kept open for the rest of the year, birds will be able to get at pests and bees will have free entry for pollination.

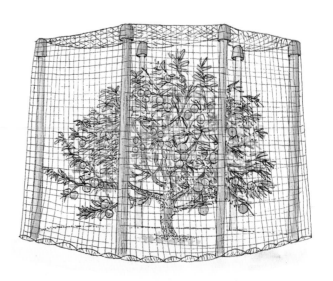

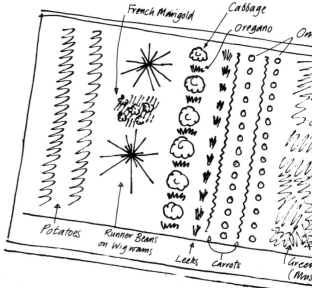

HERBS

Herbs are often used as companions of various vegetables to help ward off insect pests, but they are also one of the most used of kitchen ingredients. Traditionally they were planted near the kitchen door so that the cook could easily step out to quickly get some when they were required instead of having to tramp over a muddy garden.

WINDBREAKS

If hedges are inadequate or not yet fully mature, windbreaks can be created by planting tall-growing crops such as Jerusalem artichokes or runner beans on the windward side (right). The former are best for such situations, as runner bean plants can themselves be damaged by strong winds. Fruit bushes can also be used, gooseberries being particularly robust.

EDGING

A lot of space is wasted around the outside of vegetable gardens. It makes both visual and economic sense to line the edges of the beds with low-growing vegetables and herbs. Parsley, onions, radishes, garlic, lettuce, and even carrots can be grown as attactive edgings.

CLIMBING PLANTS

Save space by using climbing varieties of plants; they will produce more vegetables per plant in a given space than those that grow on the ground (left). Runner and French beans both have dwarf and climbing forms. Summer squash and cucumbers can also be trained up supports to take up less space. Companion plant around the base of the climbers with appropriate plants (see pages 70-71).

PLANNING

Work out the layout of your vegetable garden on paper before the season begins (left). This will ensure that you do not run out of ground and that you grow the right balance of vegetables for your needs. It is very easy in the enthusiasm of the moment to sow too many of one variety, only having to thin out later.

ROTATION OF CROPS

Rotation of crops is a very important aspect of companion planting, particularly in the vegetable garden. Since the output of a crop depends to a great extent upon nutrients within the soil, it would be advisable to arrange the different vegetables in groups which have the same nutritional requirements. If this were done then it would be easy to provide one area with manure, for instance, for those that require it and leave other garden soil untreated for those vegetables that do not have such needs.

It would seem sensible the following year to add the manure to the plot that received none the previous year and grow the demanding plants there. Sensible because if that ground were again allowed to go without the addition of nutrients, it would soon lose much of its fertility and eventually be a poor place to grow anything. The plot that received the manure the first year would by now have lost some of its fertility and would be about right for that group of plants whose requirements are more modest.

This, then, is one of the most important reasons for crop rotation: plants are grouped according to their requirements and then moved around the garden so they gain the maximum advantage from what nutrients are in that particular plot that year.

But crop rotation is not only done to match the nutritional needs of plants with the nutrients in the soil. Another reason to rotate crops is to help control pests and diseases. If the same plants are put in the same place each year, then there is likely to be a build-up of those insects and diseases that prey on those plants. On the other hand, if the plants are moved around from plot to plot within the garden, any soil-borne pests or diseases present will remain where they are without their host plants, only to perish or significantly reduce in population before their host plant is again planted there.

The rotational plan can be on a three- or four-year basis. There is normally one more plot than groups to be rotated, since there are certain plants, such as rhubarb and globe artichokes, which need a permanent position. So the fourth bed in a three-year rotation and the fifth

Extra plots can be incorporated into a garden plan to include flowering plants and herbs. Here nasturtiums (Tropaeolum majus) have been planted in the hope that they will act as a decoy and keep the nearby cabbage clear of whiteflies and cabbage moths.

THREE-YEAR ROTATION

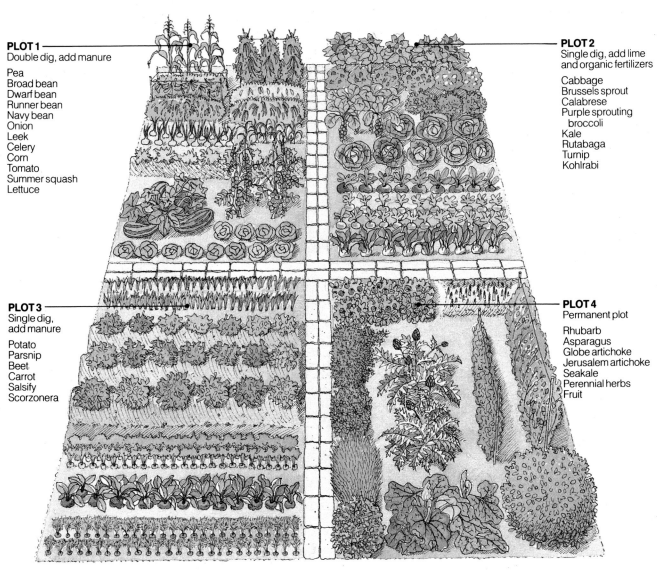

PLOT 1
Double dig, add manure

Pea
Broad bean
Dwarf bean
Runner bean
Navy bean
Onion
Leek
Celery
Corn
Tomato
Summer squash
Lettuce

PLOT 2
Single dig, add lime
and organic fertilizers

Cabbage
Brussels sprout
Calabrese
Purple sprouting
 broccoli
Kale
Rutabaga
Turnip
Kohlrabi

PLOT 3
Single dig,
add manure

Potato
Parsnip
Beet
Carrot
Salsify
Scorzonera

PLOT 4
Permanent plot

Rhubarb
Asparagus
Globe artichoke
Jerusalem artichoke
Seakale
Perennial herbs
Fruit

A three-year rotational plan, the one most commonly used, allows each plot of plants
with similar demands to change every year. This enables the plants to benefit from the
previous crop and helps to keep pest and disease populations under control. A fourth
plot is for plants that do not like to be moved.

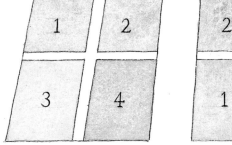
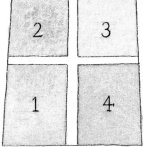
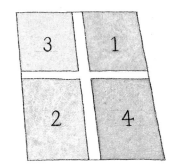

FOUR-YEAR ROTATION

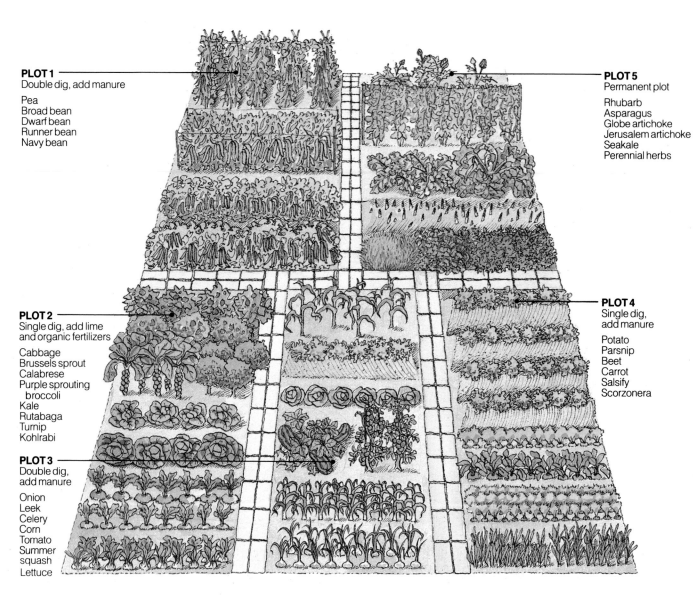

PLOT 1
Double dig, add manure

Pea
Broad bean
Dwarf bean
Runner bean
Navy bean

PLOT 2
Single dig, add lime
and organic fertilizers

Cabbage
Brussels sprout
Calabrese
Purple sprouting
 broccoli
Kale
Rutabaga
Turnip
Kohlrabi

PLOT 3
Double dig,
add manure

Onion
Leek
Celery
Corn
Tomato
Summer
squash
Lettuce

PLOT 5
Permanent plot

Rhubarb
Asparagus
Globe artichoke
Jerusalem artichoke
Seakale
Perennial herbs

PLOT 4
Single dig,
add manure

Potato
Parsnip
Beet
Carrot
Salsify
Scorzonera

*A four-year rotation plan allows the individual plots an even longer rest before the
return of a particular crop. It also gives the plots a better chance of recovering from any
pests and diseases that may have built up there the year before.*

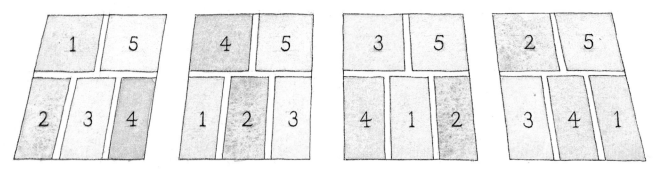

bed for a four-year rotation are reserved for this type of plant and do not rotate with the rest.

There are various alternative layouts that depend on what you want to grow, the amount of space available, and how it can be split up. However, one basic plan for a three-year rotation has in the first plot the deep-rooting vegetables that like plenty of organic material. These would include beans, peas, leeks, celery, tomatoes, and summer squash, for example. This plot should be double-dug with plenty of manure or compost added to the soil.

The second plot is reserved for the brassicas: cabbages, purple sprouting broccoli, Brussels sprouts. This plot could have incorporated in its soil some organic fertilizers such as bone meal, blood meal, and fish meal but no manure. It would also have a light dressing of lime. There is a slight problem with positioning some of the members of the family, namely rutabagas, turnips, and kohlrabi. These vegetables are usually considered root crops because of their swollen roots, even though they are closely related to the cabbages. They are susceptible to the same diseases and, on the whole, like the same conditions as the brassicas. From a nutrient point of view it does not really matter where they are planted, but from a disease point of view it is dangerous to grow brassicas on the same plot two years running.

The third plot should be single-dug, with some well-rotted manure incorporated. This is for the root crops – potatoes, parsnips, carrots, and beets – and the salad crops such as lettuces and onions.

The fourth plot is reserved for plants that only need to be changed very infrequently and are not part of the rotation. For example, asparagus, rhubarb, seakale, globe artichokes, and the perennial herbs would be found in this plot of soil.

The four-year rotation is basically the same as the three-year except an extra plot is devoted to any vegetable that is more popular than others. For example, it might be devoted entirely to potatoes or possibly to salad crops if there were a great demand for them.

The rotation plans described here and in the illustrations are only suggestions; a winter's evening can be pleasantly devoted to working out your own plan.

SOIL SICKNESS

There are several diseases known to gardeners that are little understood. Although many have been around for years there has been little economic incentive to do the work necessary to determine their cause and solution. One of these is soil sickness, sometimes known as replant sickness.

Soil sickness is most commonly found in the rose garden. If a rose bush is removed for any reason (and it need not be through ill-health or death), any rose planted in its place is liable to become sickly.

There are only two ways around this problem: plant the new rose somewhere else or dig out all the soil where the original rose bush was and replace it with fresh earth from elsewhere in the garden. This sounds easy, but it often involves moving a 10cu ft (cubic meter) or more of earth.

Soil sickness is not peculiar to shrubs; herbaceous plants suffer from it as well. The Nut Walk at Sissinghurst in Kent, England, the home and garden of the famous gardener and writer Vita Sackville-West, was once ablaze every spring with *Polyanthus*. But they dwindled to such an extent that repeated attempts to replace them were given up and other plants substituted in their place.

Vegetable gardeners may also find they have soil sickness to contend with. If tomatoes, for example, are grown every year in the same bed in a greenhouse, then the soil will need regular replacement. The tomato plants will weaken if this is not done, no matter how much fertilizer or manure is added to the soil.

The moral is not to use the same garden plan every year; for all-around good health, most plants prefer to be moved to a different location each season.

DESIGNING WITH VEGETABLES

Throughout this book we see the different possible ways of combining plants: on a rotational basis, a companionship basis, and a constant cropping basis. Any or all of these approaches can be done in an aesthetically pleasing manner so that the vegetable garden is a delight to look at and a pleasant place in which to work.

It has always seemed a strange contrast that in the cottage garden the flowers would be in the most delightful jumble, with informality being the keynote, while the vegetables would be neatly arranged in straight rows. This contrast always seems pleasing, but, as will be seen later, rows with bare earth between are a waste of a valuable resource. Closer planting results in the blurring of the rows, but the essential straightness, accentuated by the contrasting foliage, still remains.

There is no reason why shapes other than rows should not be adopted. Vegetables can be planted in square, triangular, or circular blocks, each related visually to other blocks, giving an overall pattern. This is by no means a new idea; it has been practiced on continental Europe for generations. The French *jardins potager*, or kitchen gardens, were often laid out in an elaborate manner with paths forming geometric patterns. Each bed was often edged with a low box (*Buxus sempervirens*) hedge, somewhat in the fashion of a parterre.

As long as the plantings are not too far apart this concept works well with companion planting. The different vegetables are arranged in patterns. Small hedges are a waste of productive space and can separate companionable plants, but there is no reason why edging should not be of a herb, such as parsley, or a row of lettuce, or some other vegetable. Many happy leisure hours can be spent planning both the shapes and position of the vegetables and herbs, keeping in mind their different cultural needs and how well they get on with other crops.

I think that the best-looking paths between the blocks of vegetables are those made of brick. The cheapest is beaten earth, but earth paths need a bit of maintenance to keep the weeds down. Loose stone such as gravel makes a fine looking path, but you will need some form of edging to prevent the stone from falling into the beds. Stone also has the habit of sticking to the moist soil on boots or shoes and will soon be carried all over the garden.

ABOVE *Even a small collection of vegetables on a patio or balcony can be companionably planted, as demonstrated here.*

LEFT *Knot gardens, made from low hedges, make ideal decorative enclosures in which to grow herbs. Here box (*Buxus sempervirens*) and santolina (*Santolina chamaecyparissus) have been used to give contrast in color and texture.*

RIGHT *This French parterre incorporates both vegetables and flowers in an extremely decorative, as well as practical, manner.*

PROTECTING CROPS

A great number of chemicals can now be used to protect crops, but it is quite possible to avoid them by invoking nature's help.

INSECTIVOROUS PLANTS

A novel way of helping to keep insects in check is by trapping them with insectivorous (insect-eating) plants, such as the pitcher plant *(Nepenthes)* shown left. This is not practical nor really possible in the open garden because a great number of such plants would be needed, but in a greenhouse a few plants in pots will help to keep pests under control. They attack all insects whether good or bad, so cannot be considered the ultimate defense against pests. A regular examination of the plants will show what insects they are digesting, which will give a good indication of the pests and their levels in the greenhouse and whether any other pest control action is needed. Insectivorous plants, as well as being useful, have their own curious charm.

INSECT TRAPS

It is not always easy to tell what insect pests there are around, particularly if you are away at work all day. A yellow dish filled with water will attract insects and then drown them, giving a good indication of what pests there are and in what numbers. This technique is particularly useful in greenhouses.

SOME OF THE PESTS TO LOOK OUT FOR

Pest	Host
Blackfly	Bean
Carrot root fly	Carrot, parsnip
Caterpillar	Cabbage
Colorado beetle	Potato
Nematode	Squash family, potato
Flea beetle	Cabbage
Greenfly (aphid)	Most vegetables
Onion fly	Onion
Slug	Most vegetables
Whitefly	Cabbage

DISEASE RESISTANCE

Many plants have a greater natural resistance to pests and diseases than others. Many of the older varieties of both vegetables and flowering plants have come down to us by the very virtue of their being tougher and able to survive. Modern plant breeding has bred a lot of different characteristics into plants, many at the expense of disease resistance. On the other hand they have also improved some varieties. Look carefully at the seed catalogues and choose those vegetables which have a greater resistance to such diseases as mildew (part of a page from a catologue is reproduced right). For flowering plants watch out for many of the older cottage garden plants; they might not be quite as spectacular as some of their modern counterparts, but they will be tougher.

Healthy plants, such as the luscious-looking peas shown right, are more resistant to disease and pests than those which are undernourished and in poor condition.

casseroles, flavouring sauces, gravies, serving with fish dishes and pickling. Store for nearly 12 months.
LT202   Dutch Yellow (approx. ½ lb. when packed)

TREE ONIONS
LT994   Egyptian Tree Onions Ht. 24—36in.
A very unusual onion that forms bulblets up to the size of Walnuts at the top of the stem (instead of seed). Their flavour is crispy and spicy and they are delicious pickled. They are very hardy, immune to onion fly, easy to grow and will continue to crop year after year. (Illust.) (10 bulblets)

ONIONS FROM SEED
How to grow
Provide lots of compost or fertiliser to your soil. Sow the seed in March/April in 9in. spaced rows, ½ in. deep, and thin out to 6in. apart for autumn harvest. One packet will sow a row

BIOLOGICAL CONTROL

Biological control is increasingly being used to combat pests. Some botanic gardens have gone over entirely to this form of defense. It involves releasing a predator which proceeds to eat the pests. For example it is possible to purchase ladybugs and lacewings to help fight outbreaks of aphids. There are many more sophisticated predators available to control a large range of pests.

PLANTS THAT REPEL INSECTS

Chemical science has developed so fast that few people stop to question the necessity of many of its products. At the first sight of a bug, out comes the insecticidal spray and the insect, good or bad, is sent into oblivion. If all insects are harmful, how have plants managed to survive over the thousands of years of their existence? The answer, of course, is that all insects are not harmful. As a matter of fact, most insects do neither harm nor good, and some are actually beneficial to plants. It is the relatively few insect pests that we humans are concerned about.

In the past we used our native intelligence to help nature combat nature, so to speak. In this century we have learned how to "improve upon" nature, with chemicals. At first agricultural chemicals seemed like the answer to most of our crop problems. Now we know that the long-term problems that some create are not worth their short-term benefits. So we are taking another look at the gentler approaches we used in the past.

Most of the plant protection methods of the past were developed through personal experience rather than by means of carefully controlled experiments. Many things were tried and those that were successful in controlling pests were passed on; many are still used today. Some agrochemists pooh-pooh such methods to control pests and label them as nothing more than folklore. But like a lot of folklore, such gardening lore is based on a great deal of true experience.

The gardening lore I am speaking of is the use of certain plants to control pests that bother other plants. It is one important part of the companion planting concept. Particular plants can protect their neighbors, for example, by masking the smell of a plant vulnerable to attack, deter the predators or poison them, or lure them off to other feeding grounds.

Such protection capabilities of a few plants are well known in gardening lore and are accepted as fact by many experienced gardeners. Claims about other plants, however, are more controversial. What works for some gardeners does not seem to work for others. What works one year may not work the next. So many factors are at play: different soil composition and conditions, whether there is a hedge nearby, the varieties of plants in the garden, the time of year each is planted, what other insects or animals are around, weather conditions, and so on. Laboratories can prove that certain plants

The benefits of planting onions and carrots together have long been known by gardeners. The onions help keep the carrot root fly away from the carrots, and the carrots do their part by keeping the onion fly from attacking the onions.

contain insecticides but cannot tell us whether the plant uses them or whether they are effective under normal growing conditions.

Some supposedly effective measures rely on chance encounters, a bit like keeping elephants out of the garden by hanging an orange in a tree: there are no elephants so it must work. The reduction of aphids on one plant one year might not be due to some property of a neighboring plant, but rather to the unseen fact that there were more ladybugs around, or indeed, less aphids in the first place.

This year by accident rather than design I planted celery next to some brassicas in my garden. While researching for this book I discovered that celery is supposed to keep white butterflies away from cabbages, but my cabbage had been damaged by the larvae of the butterflies, somewhat disproving the theory. But did it? In another vegetable plot a hundred yards away, the brassicas had been reduced to tatters by the butterfly larvae, whereas in the first, by the celery, the cabbage had only been nibbled at.

The most popular plant protection technique in companion planting is using one plant to deter the predators of a neighboring plant. One of many proven examples of this is the use of French marigolds (*Tagetes patula*) to reduce the numbers of Mexican bean beetles.

In a few cases the insects are actually killed by the companion plants. For example, the black nightshade (*Solanum nigrum*) attracts Colorado beetles and they lay their eggs close by. When the larvae hatch, they eat the poisonous plant and perish, thus reducing the number of beetles that prey on nearby potatoes. A similar sequence of events happens to Colorado beetles with the Jimson-weed, or thorn apple (*Datura stramonium*).

Marigolds have a similar effect and can be used for clearing the ground of various destructive nematodes. African and French marigolds will both attract nematodes into their roots where they are unable to breed, thus effectively reducing the next generation of nematodes. Using marigolds for this purpose is most effective if the flowers are planted heavily in an area a season before planting the desired crops. Less effective, but still worth trying is to interplant the marigolds with the

*Claims have been made for the sunflower (*Helianthus annuus*) as an alternative food source for stinkbugs and corn earworms, thus reducing their numbers elsewhere. But their main use in the garden is as a host to hoverflies and predatory wasps.*

53

main crop as it grows. Castor beans (*Ricinus communis*) can be used in much the same way to control nematodes.

Another way in which plants can be used to combat insect infestation – by masking plants – is long established. There are claims that many aromatic herbs and vegetables can effectively be used to disguise the smell of their neighbors. Carrot flies are attracted to their hosts by the carrot's smell, and it has long been practice to interplant them with onions whose own smell effectively confuses the flies.

In many cases the companion plant physically disguises the host plant. It has been proven, for example, that a cover crop of clover makes it difficult for cabbage root flies to get to the roots of the cabbage. A closely planted area makes it more difficult for insects to find their target plants, and a mixed garden of this nature is likely to have the best results in keeping pest numbers to a reasonable proportion.

Other plants can be interplanted in a garden as decoys. Many gardeners claim that fat hen, or lamb's-quarters (*Chenopodium album*) will attract leafminers away from other plants. And they believe that it has the added benefit of being attractive to ladybugs which prey on the leafminers.

Whatever specific interplantings you use, there is no doubt that a mixed garden will contain less troublesome pests than one with restricted plantings. Because there is a greater diversity of plants there will be a greater number of different pests, with less chance for any one pest to build up to a dangerous population level.

*Garden lore has long claimed that marigolds (*Tagetes*) repel many types of insects. Research is now attempting to show precisely what these plants can and cannot achieve. But their use in reducing nematodes in the soil is already well proven.*

DECOY PLANTS

Some plants act as alternative food sources for pests, distracting them away from the main crop plant. Careful placement of these decoy plants is necessary, otherwise they may do just the opposite of what is intended and entice the pests onto the main crops.

Plants	Insects they attract
Alfalfa, or lucerne *Medicago sativa*	lygus bugs
Black nightshade *Solanum nigrum*	Colorado beetles
Fat hen, or lamb's quarters *Chenopodium album*	leafminers
Hyssop *Hyssopus officinalis*	cabbage butterflies
Jimsonweed, or thorn apple *Datura stramonium*	Colorado beetles
Mustard *Brassica nigra*	cabbage butterflies

SOME PESTS TO LOOK OUT FOR

 **Carrot root fly**
The maggot of this fly tunnels into the roots of carrots and parsnips, destroying their value.

 Cabbage moth
The moth lays its eggs on cabbages. These hatch into caterpillars, which eat the leaves.

 **Onion fly**
The maggot of this fly burrows into the base of the bulbs, killing it or severely retarding its growth.

 Diamond-back moth
The larvae of this moth eat the underside of cabbage leaves, making silver-looking holes.

 Cabbage whitefly
This moth and its larvae eat the undersides of cabbage leaves. Honeydew and sooty molds develop.

 **Black bean aphid**
This fly attacks the succulent shoots of broad beans, weakening the plant and distorting the growing pods.

 **Slug**
The slug eats nearly all vegetable material, including roots below ground. Few vegetables seem immune to it.

 **Snail**
The snail has the same diet as the slug, except it forages mainly above ground. Green vegetables are particularly at risk.

 Colorado beetle
This beetle attacks potato crops.

PLANT DISTRESS
SIGNALS

Vegetable	Symptom	Cause
Bean	stunted growth and obvious signs of blackfly notches eaten from margins of leaves	black bean aphids weevils
Beet	blotches or blisters on the leaves	leafminers
Cabbage	small holes in leaves large holes in leaves silvery holes on underside of the leaves yellowing, curling leaves with waxy, gray insects weakening plants with sooty molds, honeydew, and obvious signs of whitefly wilting leaves and tunneled roots wilting leaves and tunneled stems	flea beetles caterpillars or slugs diamond-back moths mealy aphids cabbage whiteflies cabbage root flies flea beetles
Carrot	tunneling in the roots, wilting leaves, turning yellow	carrot root flies
Celery	blotches or blisters on the leaves	celery leafminers
Cucumber	yellowing and nodules on the roots holes in the cucumber	nematodes slugs or snails
Lettuce	holes in leaves stunted growth, yellowing leaves, white powdery patches on roots stunted growth, yellowing leaves, lumps on the roots sticky honeydew and obvious signs of aphids	slugs or snails root aphids nematodes greenflies
Onion	leaves drooping, turning yellow swollen and distorted leaves	onion flies nematodes
Parsnip	tunneling in the roots, wilting leaves, turning yellow	carrot flies
Pea	silvery patches on leaves and pods notches eaten from margins of leaves stunted growth and obvious signs of greenfly on stems	thrips weevils greenflies
Potato	browning leaves and obvious signs of aphids brown spots and holes in leaves weak and stunted plants with dying lower leaves small holes and tunnels in tubers large holes in tubers leaves eaten, black excreta, and obvious signs of black and yellow beetles and their red larvae	greenflies capsid bugs nematodes wireworms slugs Colorado beetles
Summer squash	yellowing and nodules on the roots holes in the summer squash	nematodes slugs, snails, or mice
Tomato	stunted growth and wilted leaves, lumps on the roots stunted and curled leaves, sticky honeydew holes in fruit	nematodes whiteflies slugs

PEST DETERRENTS – A SUMMARY

One alternative to using pesticides is to use plants that repel, kill, or otherwise deter pests. Over the centuries many claims have been made about specific plants that control specific pests, but little so far has been scientifically proven. Modern research has not yet determined just what works and under what conditions, so some experimenting in your own garden is the only way you can find out what plants can actually provide you with some protection against pests.

Plant name	Claimed effects
African marigold *Tagetes erecta*	reduces nematodes
Anise *Pimpinella anisum*	deters aphids, fleas, reduces cabbage worms
Alfalfa, or lucerne *Medicago sativa*	reduces corn wireworms
Basil *Ocimum basilicum*	controls variety of pests
Bean *Phaseolus*	reduces corn armyworms
Black nightshade *Solanum nigrum*	reduces Colorado beetles
Borage *Borage officinalis*	attracts bees, reduces Japanese beetles on potatoes, and deters tomato hornworms
Broccoli *Brassica oleacea*	reduces striped cucumber beetles
Caper spurge *Euphorbia lathyrus*	deters moles
Carrot *Daucus carota*	deters onion flies
Castor bean *Ricinus communis*	controls moles, mosquitoes, and nematodes
Catnip *Nepeta cataria*	deters ants, aphids, Colorado beetles, darkling beetles, flea beetles, Japanese beetles, squash bugs, weevils
Celery *Apium graveolens*	deters cabbage butterflies
Chive *Allium schoenoprasum*	cures blackspot on roses, deters Japanese beetles, discourages insects climbing fruit trees
Chrysanthemum *Chrysanthemum coccineum*	reduces nematodes
Clover *Trifolium*	deters cabbage root flies
Coriander *Coriandrum sativum*	deters Colorado beetles
Corn *Zea mays*	reduces striped cucumber beetles
Dandelion *Taraxacum officinale*	repels Colorado beetles
Dead nettle *Lamium album*	deters potato bugs
Dill *Anethum graveolens*	repels aphids and spider mites
Elderberry *Sambucus*	general insect repellent
Eucalyptus *Eucalyptus*	general insect repellent
Fennel *Foeniculum vulgare*	deters aphids
French marigold *Tagetes patula*	deters Mexican bean beetles, nematodes
Garlic *Allium sativum*	general insect repellent, deters Japanese beetles

Plant name	Claimed effects
Horseradish *Armoracia rusticana*	deters Colorado beetles
Hyssop *Hyssopus officinalis*	repels flea beetles, insect larvae
Jimsonweed, or thorn apple *Datura stramonium*	reduces Colorado beetles
Johnson grass *Sorghum halepense*	reduces Willamette mites on vines
Lavender cotton *Santolina chamaecyparissus*	deters corn wireworms and southern rootworms
Leek *Allium ampeloprasum*	deters carrot flies
Marigold *Tagetes*	reduces nematodes, cabbage pests
Milkweed *Asclepias*	deters aphids
Mustard *Brassica nigra*	reduces aphids
Nasturtium *Tropaeolum majus*	reduces aphids, cabbage worms, Colorado beetles, deters squash bugs and whiteflies
Onion *Allium cepa*	deters Colorado beetles, carrot flies
Peanut *Arachis hypogaea*	deters *Ostrinia furnacalis*
Petunia *Petunia*	repels Mexican bean beetles, potato bugs, and squash bugs
Pot marigold *Calendula officinalis*	deters asparagus beetles, tomato hornworms
Potato *Solanum tuberosum*	deters Mexican bean beetles
Radish *Raphanus sativus*	deters cucumber beetles, root flies, vine borers, and many other pests
Ragweed *Ambrosia artemisiifolia*	reduces flea beetles
Rue *Ruta graveolens*	deters beetles and fleas
Rosemary *Rosmarinus officinalis*	deters bean beetles, cabbage moths, carrot flies, and many other insects
Rye *Secale*	reduces nematodes
Sage *Salvia officinalis*	deters cabbage worms, cabbage moths, and root maggots
Savory *Satureja*	deters Mexican bean beetles
Scorzonera *Scorzonera hispanica*	deters carrot flies
Southernwood *Artemisia abrotanum*	deters cabbage moths, carrot flies
Soybean *Glycine max*	deters corn earworms, corn borers
Spurry *Spergula arvensis*	reduces aphids, caterpillars, and root worms
Sudan grass *Sorghum sudanense*	reduces Willamette mites on vines
Tansy *Tanecetum vulgare*	deters many insects including ants, aphids, cabbage worms, Colorado beetles, Japanese beetles, squash bugs
Thyme *Thymus vulgaris*	deters cabbage loopers, cabbage worms, whiteflies
Tomato *Lycopersicon lycopersicum*	deters loopers, flea beetles, and whiteflies on cabbage
Wormwood *Artemisia*	general insecticide; deters mice and other rodents, slugs, and snails

PREDATORS AND NATURAL ENEMIES

One of the ways that Nature keeps pests under control is by providing other insects which live on them. Aphids (greenflies and black-flies) are some of the most frequently seen pests, but as soon as a serious outbreak occurs there is usually a natural increase in the number of ladybugs nearby. They lay their eggs and when the young ladybugs hatch they eat the aphids. Lacewings and hoverflies are two other insects that prey on aphids.

Rather than wait for a large outbreak of aphids to increase their numbers, ladybugs, lacewings, and hoverflies can be enticed to the garden by other plantings. Most of these predatory insects need plants rich in nectar and pollen to supplement their diet of aphids. If these plants are provided then the predators will usually be around in sufficient numbers to keep the greenfly and blackfly populations under control.

Fortunately there is a wide range of plants that insects as well as gardeners find attractive. Examples include the various sunflowers (*Helianthus*), fennel (*Foeniculum vulgare*), goldenrod (*Solidago*), or herbs, such as hyssop (*Hyssopus officinalis*) or mint. A border made up of such flowers will attract hoverflies and other aphid-eating insects and it will provide the garden with much color. Wild flowers are especially attractive to these insects,

and the base of a hedgerow or orchard planted with them is most beneficial.

It is, of course, not only aphids that are controlled in such a way. Lacewings will eat caterpillars, corn ear-worms, leafhoppers, mealybugs, mites, and a host of other pests. Blackberries act as hosts to a parasite of the grape leafhopper, which does much damage to grape vines. The presence of blackberry bushes around the edge of the vineyard encourages the growth of a population of parasites sufficient enough to control the leafhoppers. Spurry (*Spergula arvensis*) similarly plays host to parasites and predators which help to control cabbage worm.

Predators not only need alternative food sources, they need shelter as well. Lacewings find shelter in ever-greens and the tree of heaven (*Ailanthus altissima*), while a parasite of the diamondback moth overwinters in hawthorn.

Greater diversity of plants in the garden increases the number of insects present, and research has shown that under such circumstances it is always the predators which stay on top.

Above *Lacewings and their larvae prey on some of the most common pests. Their presence in the garden will substantially reduce the numbers of greenflies and blackflies.*

Right *Hoverflies, here seen extracting nectar, live off quite a number of pests, including aphids. The more flowering plants in the garden that attract these beneficial insects, the better.*

Ladybug larvae feed hungrily on greenfly, blackfly, and other related species. The presence of ladybugs in the garden will help keep their populations under control.

HOSTS TO INSECTS

Many of the predators that live off insect pests can be attracted to the garden by incorporating in it plants that they like. Their presence will never rid the garden of pests, but it will help to keep them at tolerable levels.

Plant name	Insect
Amaranth (Pigweed) *Amaranthus*	ground beetles
Anise *Pimpinella anisum*	beneficial wasps
Blackberry *Rubus*	*Anagrus epos*
Celery (flowers) *Apium graveolens*	beneficial wasps
Chamomile *Chamaemelum nobile*	hoverflies, beneficial wasps
Chervil *Anthriscus cerefolium*	hoverflies, beneficial wasps, and others
Clover *Trifolium*	ground beetles, parasites of woolly apple aphids
Dandelion *Taraxacum officinale*	beneficial wasps
Fennel *Foeniculum vulgare*	hoverflies, beneficial wasps
Goldenrod *Solidago*	hoverflies, praying mantis, and other predators
Hawthorn *Crataegus*	diamondback moth parasites
Hyssop *Hyssopus officinalis*	hoverflies, beneficial wasps, and others
Ivy *Hedera helix*	hoverflies and beneficial wasps
Marigold *Tagetes*	hoverflies
Milkweed *Asclepias*	several parasites
Mint *Mentha*	hoverflies, and several wasps and other beneficial insects
Mustard *Brassica hirta*	various parasites
Peanut *Arachis hypogaea*	predatory spiders on *Ostrinia furnacalis*
Ragweed *Ambrosia*	parasites for oriental fruit moths and strawberry leaf rollers
Soybean *Glycine max*	trichogramma wasps
Spurry *Spergula arvensis*	several insects that prey on cabbage pests
Stinging nettle *Urtica dioica*	many beneficial insects
Strawberry *Fragaria*	parasites of the oriental fruit moth
Sunflower *Helianthus*	lacewings, beneficial wasps
Tansy *Tanacetum vulgare*	ladybugs
Yarrow *Achillea*	ladybugs, predatory wasps

PLANTS THAT FIGHT BACK

Nature has several ways of keeping the balance between predators and prey. We have already seen that one of the ways Nature accomplishes this is by making sure that the predators in turn also have predators, thus aphids are eaten by lacewings. Another way is for the plant to fight back by producing a toxin that is either unpalatable or poisonous to its predator.

Many plants contain toxins of various kinds. Often it is in small quantities so that it does not actually poison the insect, but makes it move on to other plants. When eaten, the leaves of potatoes produce a poison that discourages the preying insect from eating too much of it; instead it moves on to another plant that has not yet been attacked. In this way the damage is limited. Some plants have taken this a step further; when one plant is attacked it sets off a response in neighboring plants which triggers these plants to produce the deterring toxin themselves before the insect moves on to feast upon them. Unfortunately the plants that so far have been found to have this response mechanism are of no garden value, but in time, doubtless, this response will be bred into plants for our use.

Some plants produce substances which are downright poisons, and these can be extracted and used as insecticides. Sprays and emulsions of various types have been used for centuries. Pyrethrum is a good example of an insecticide still produced commercially from extracts of various species of *Chrysanthemum*. Some such as nicotine, derived from tobacco plants (*Nicotiana*), are extremely poisonous and although natural poisons, they are indiscriminate and will kill beneficial insects as well as pests.

Other, less toxic sprays, have been produced by gardeners for their own use. Garlic has traditionally been used in a spray form for deterring aphids, codling moth, and rusts.

The predators of plants are not only insects and other animals; other plants (namely weeds in gardens) often crowd them out, starving them of food and light. The response in many cases is the same as with insects: the plant's release of poisons.

It starts at an early stage in the plant's life when many seeds release toxic substances to inhibit the germination of other seeds around them. At later stages of development, the roots of the plant emit chemicals that restrict the growth of specific plants or of all plants with which they come into contact within the immediate neighborhood. This process is known as alleopathy.

In some cases the alleopathic emissions are so strong that they kill virtually everything around them. Black walnut (*Juglans nigra*), for example, produces the toxin juglone, which it emits through its roots. This toxin is so strong that many plants that come in contact with it wilt or die.

Much scientific research is going into using these natural herbicides in a more deliberate way. At the moment it is mainly farmers that are benefiting, but some of their techniques are suitable for gardeners, too. For example, it has been discovered that some crops that are used as cover crops, such as rye and wheat, contain alleopathic qualities that help reduce weed competition. If one of these plants is sowed in advance of the main crop, it will reduce the number of broadleaf weeds emerging in the field or garden. Then, if this cover crop is cut 30 to 50 days after germination and allowed to wilt, the cut stems and foliage will give additional cover for a few weeks until the main crop is established.

Unfortunately, using a plant as a companion just because of its alleopathic ability may not be wise. Sometimes its power can be a bit indiscriminate, reducing the vigor of other crops as well as weeds, sometimes to the detriment of other benefits. And sometimes a plant's alleopathic benefit is offset by a negative characteristic. Anise (*Pimpinella anisum*), for example, is known to reduce the number of cabbage worms when planted next to cabbages, but it also reduces the yield of the cabbages.

How plants help and hinder other plants is a fascinating science still in its early stages. Much research is still needed to clarify which plants contain harmful and which beneficial substances and how these can be best used.

Over the years gardening lore has made many claims about the good and bad effects of plants on each other's growth. The tables starting on page 70 summarize some of the beneficial claims that have been made.

A general insecticide spray can be made by boiling rhubarb leaves in water for half an hour and then straining off the liquid. Rhubarb spray is very poisonous so use it with care.

SPRAYS AND OILS
PRODUCED FROM PLANTS

RIGHT Chrysanthemum coccineum *has been used by manufacturers to make the non-persistent insecticide pyrethrum (though you should not attempt to make this spray yourself). The living plant is harmless to insects.*

BELOW *Always exercise extreme caution when making up sprays. Use utensils you have earmarked especially for the purpose. Do not eat sprayed plants for at least two weeks.*

1 *The leaves of the plant can be shredded and steeped in boiling water.*

2 *Leave for an hour or so and then emulsify by pushing the leaves and water through a very fine sieve or by pulverizing in an electric blender.*

3 *To help it stick to the plant add some soapflakes to the solution. Then spray it on the infected plant.*

Warning: all sprays are dangerous. Those made from plants are generally less so than manufactured chemicals. Nevertheless you should *not* make up solutions of nicotine (tobacco) or chrysanthemum – though manufacturers use these as a base for commercial insecticides – or any other plants the properties of which you are uncertain. All sprays should be used with extreme caution and only when all other methods of control have failed. When preparing your own sprays do not use the kitchen blender or other kitchen utensils unless specifically reserved for this purpose. Do not eat sprayed plants for at least two weeks.

Plant name	Control for
Basil *Ocimum basilicum*	aphids, asparagus beetles
Catnip *Nepeta cataria*	Colorado beetles
Chestnut *Castanea sativa*	beet moths
Chive *Allium schoenoprasum*	apple scab, mildew on cucumbers, gooseberries, summer squash and pumpkins
Citrus fruit *Citrus*	fall armyworms and bollworms
Coriander *Coriandrum sativum*	aphids, spider mites
Elderberry *Sambucus*	aphids, carrot flies, cucumber beetles, peach tree borers, root maggots
Eucalyptus *Eucalyptus*	general insecticide
Garlic *Allium sativum*	against a whole range of pests including aphids, caterpillars, codling moths, Japanese beetles, root maggots, rusts, snails
Horseradish *Armoracia rusticana*	fungicide for fruit trees
Horsetail *Equisetum*	slugs and snails
Ivy *Hedera helix*	corn wireworms
Mint *Mentha*	Colorado beetles, ants
Parsley *Petroselinum crispum*	asparagus beetles
Pelargonium *Pelargonium*	cabbage moths, corn earworms, and Japanese beetles
Pepper *Capsicum*	general insect repellent
Rhubarb *Rheum rhabarbarum*	general insecticide, blackspot
Johnson grass *Sorghum halepense*	Willamette mites on vines
Sage *Salvia officinalis*	cabbage worms
Southernwood *Artemisia abrotanum*	cabbage worms
Thyme *Thymus vulgaris*	cabbage worms
Tomato *Lycopersicon lycopersicum*	asparagus beetles
Wormwood *Artemisia*	fleas

KEEPING THE GROUND COVERED

One of the most attractive sights in a garden is the neat, straight rows of vegetables alternating with lines of bare earth carefuly tilled and free of weeds. Attractive as this may be, the sight of bare earth is becoming an anathema to many gardeners, particularly those with small gardens. Bare earth is under-utilized garden space.

Intercropping and successional cropping are two important techniques for getting maximum use out of your garden. Intercropping involves planting fast-growing plants in areas that will eventually be taken up by larger but slower-growing vegetables. A good example of this is growing lettuces between rows of cabbages. Cabbages, because of their size, need to be planted 1-2ft (30-60cm) apart depending on the variety. While they are still young much of the space between them is bare; planting a row or patch of lettuce there fills this space quickly. By the time the cabbages begin to cover the ground, the lettuces will have matured and been lifted.

It is also possible to intercrop within a row. Parsnips, for example, are slow in germinating. But if some radish seed is mixed in with it at sowing time then these germinate first and can be cleared before the parsnips have reached any size at all. So you get two crops from the same space. In addition, the fast-growing radishes sprout early and act as a marker in the row for the slower-growing parsnips, allowing the soil to be hoed without fear of the hoe unknowingly wandering into the row with the germinating seed.

This not only makes better use of the ground, it also keeps the ground covered, which helps suppress weeds and reduce the weather's drying and possibly eroding effects on the soil. Plants should never be planted so closely that they exclude light from one another. Light is essential for growth, and plants will strive to get to it if they possibly can. Too close a planting will result in plants becoming drawn and spindly as they struggle to reach up toward it.

One successful planting technique is to plant one crop immediately after the ground is cleared of another. In some cases the second can be planted before the first is harvested. Young cabbage plants, for example, can be planted between rows of shallots as the latter finish maturing. The shallots will be removed before the cabbages start to grow. Another successional planting technique is to sow rows of the same crop at two weekly intervals so that they do not all mature at the same time. This avoids having a glut of one vegetable followed by a lull when there is nothing to harvest.

If there is time between crops when the ground is not needed for planting a vegetable, sow mustard or some other green manure as described on pages 22-23.

It will be some time before these cabbages and curly kale will fill the space allotted to them. In the meantime two varieties of lettuce have been planted here, both to produce another crop and to cover the ground so that the weeds are kept at bay.

Here is a good example of companion planting, with all the available space between the cabbages and leeks taken up by masses of herbs. Such interplanting makes good sense, not only because it gets the maximum use from the space, but because it also helps keep weeds down and makes the garden a very attractive place in which to be.

NOTES ON HERB AND VEGETABLE ASSOCIATIONS

Vegetables and herbs are not difficult to grow, yet the rewards are great. Growing them together and with the right companions improves the chances of a good crop.

INVASIVE HERBS

Some herbs, mint for example, are very invasive, spreading by underground runners. They make good companions, but their invasiveness restricts their use. However, their rambling tendencies can be curbed if such herbs are planted in a container, for example an old oil drum or old bucket, which has had the bottom removed and then sunk into the earth with its rim level with the ground. Another way is to put the herb in a conventional container and stand it among the other vegetables and herbs.

LIGHT

All plants must have light reaching their leaves in order to produce carbohydrates on which they live. Plants that do not get enough grow spindly and are sickly looking. Be careful when selecting and planting companion plants that they do not exclude light from each other. Most vegetables need full sun. A few, listed here, will tolerate partial shade, however, they must have direct sunlight for part of the day.

Asparagus, broccoli, Brussels sprout, cabbage, carrot, celeriac, celery, cress, cucumber, garlic, kale, kohlrabi, leek, lettuce, onion, parsley, parsnip, spinach, Swiss chard, turnip.

broccoli

spinach

celeriac

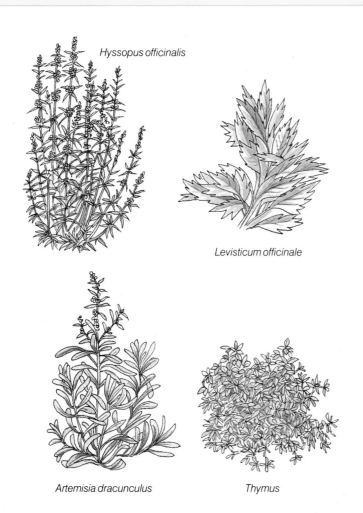

Hyssopus officinalis

Levisticum officinale

Origanum majorana

Artemisia dracunculus

Thymus

BENEFICIAL HERBS

Some herbs seem to have a beneficial presence in the garden and go with nearly all other vegetables and herbs. Below are listed a few of these.

Hyssop *Hyssopus officinalis*
Lovage *Levisticum officinale*
Marjoram *Origanum majorana*
Tarragon *Artemisia dracunculus*
Thyme *Thymus*
Yarrow *Achillea*

OTHER COMPANIONS

Not all companion plants are normally grown in the garden. Some fodder crops or even wild plants are useful for fixing nitrogen in the soil. They can be used as green manure (see pages 22-23), or, since they will not overrun the garden, as companion plants among the vegetables. The following are worth considering:

Alfalfa or lucerne *Medicago sativa*
Bird's foot trefoil *Lotus corniculatus*
Lupin *Lupinus* (see right)
Red clover *Trifolium pratense*
Sainfoin *Onobrychis viciifolia*
Vetch *Vicia*
White clover *Trifolium repens*

VEGETABLES AND THEIR COMPANIONS

Here is a list of vegetables with what many gardeners believe to be their good and poor companions – other plants which are claimed to be beneficial or detrimental to their growth and well-being. Gardening lore suggests planting them together to enhance their growth or flavor, or to protect them from pests and diseases. Research has proved that some of these claims are justified, others await proof or disproof.

Vegetable	Good companions	Poor companions
Asparagus *Asparagus officinalis*	parsley, tomato	onion
Bean *Phaseolus vulgaris* *Vicia faba*	beet, borage, cabbage, carrot, cauliflower, corn, marigold, squash, strawberry, tomato	chive, fennel, garlic, leek
Beet *Beta vulgaris*	cabbage, kohlrabi	runner bean
Broccoli *Brassica oleracea*	bean, celery, chamomile, dill, mint, nasturtium, onion, oregano, potato, sage, rosemary	lettuce, strawberry, tomato
Brussels sprout *Brassica oleracea*	bean, celery, dill, hyssop, mint, nasturtium, potato, sage, rosemary	strawberry
Cabbage *Brassica oleracea*	bean, beet, celery, chamomile, dill, hyssop, mint, nasturtium, onion, oregano, potato, sage, rosemary	grape, strawberry, tomato
Carrot *Daucus carota*	bean, leek, onion, pea, radish, rosemary, sage, scorzonera, tomato, wormwood	dill
Cauliflower *Brassica oleracea*	bean, beet, celery, chamomile, dill, hyssop, mint, nasturtium, onion, oregano, potato, sage, radish	strawberry, tomato
Celeriac *Apium graveolens*	bean, cabbage, leek, onion, tomato	
Celery *Apium graveolens*	bean, cabbage, leek, onion, tomato	
Corn *Zea mays*	bean, lupin, melon, pea, squash	
Cucumber *Cucumis sativus*	bean, broccoli, celery, Chinese cabbage, lettuce, pea, radish, tomato	rue, sage
Eggplant *Solanum melongena*	pea, tarragon, thyme	
Horseradish *Armoracia rusticana*	potato	
Kohlrabi *Brassica oleracea*	beet, onion	bean, pepper, tomato
Leek *Allium porrum*	carrot, celeriac, celery	broad bean, broccoli
Lettuce *Lactuca sativa*	beet, cabbage, clover, pea, radish, strawberry	
Melon *Cucumis melo*	corn, peanut, sunflower	
Onion *Allium cepa*	beet, cabbage, carrot, lettuce, potato, strawberry, tomato	bean, pea

Vegetable	Good companions	Poor companions
Pea *Pisum sativum*	carrot, corn, cucumber, eggplant, lettuce, radish, spinach, tomato, turnip	
Pepper *Capsicum*	basil, carrot, lovage, marjoram, onion, oregano	fennel, kohlrabi
Potato *Solanum tuberosum*	bean, cabbage, corn, lettuce, onion, petunia, marigold, radish	apple, pumpkin, tomato
Pumpkin *Cucurbita moschata*	bean, corn, mint, nasturtium, radish	potato
Radish *Raphanus sativus*	bean, cabbage, cauliflower, cucumber, lettuce, pea, squash, tomato	grape, hyssop
Spinach *Oleracea*	cabbage, celery, eggplant, onion, pea, strawberry	
Squash *Cucurbita moschata*	bean, corn, mint, nasturtium, radish	
Summer squash *Cucurbita pepo*	bean, corn, mint, nasturtium, radish	potato
Tomato *Lycopersicon lycopersicum*	asparagus, basil, cabbage, carrot, onion, parsley, pea, sage	fennel, potato
Turnip *Brassica rapa*	pea	
Zucchini *Cucurbita pepo*	bean, corn, mint, nasturtium, radish	potato

Beans and cabbage are reputed to be good companions, each increasing the other's yields. Here (above) French beans are grown with one of the cabbages. Summer squash and corn (right) are also classic companions which can be intercropped.

HERBS AND THEIR COMPANIONS

H erbs can be beneficial to a large range of other herbs and vegetables. Claimed companions improve the performance or taste as well as keep predators away. On the other hand, poor companions can be detrimental to associated plants growing close by. The list below shows a range of herbs and those plants which are said to be their good and bad companions.

Herb	Good companions	Poor companions
Anise *Pimpinella anisum*	bean, coriander	carrot
Basil *Ocimum basilicum*	bean, cabbage, tomato	rue
Borage *Borago officinalis*	strawberry, tomato	
Caraway *Carum carvi*	pea	fennel
Chamomile *Chamaemelum nobile*	cucumber, mint, onion	
Chervil *Anthriscus cerefolium*	carrot, radish	
Chive *Allium schoenoprasum*	carrot, grape, parsley, tomato	bean, pea
Coriander *Coriandrum sativum*	anise, potato	fennel
Dill *Anethum graveolens*	cabbage, lettuce, onion	carrot, tomato
Fennel *Foeniculum vulgare*		bean, caraway, coriander, dill, tomato
Garlic *Allium sativum*	carrot, rose, tomato	bean, pea, strawberry
Hyssop *Hyssopus officinalis*	cabbage, grape, plants in general	radish
Lemon balm *Melissa officinalis*	tomato	
Lovage *Levisticum officinale*	bean	
Marjoram *Origanum majorana*	plants in general	
Mint *Mentha*	cabbage, plants in general	parsley
Oregano *Origanum vulgare*	cabbage, cucumber	
Parsley *Petroselinum crispum*	asparagus, carrot, chive, tomato	mint
Rosemary *Rosmarinus officinalis*	bean, cabbage, carrot	potato
Rue *Ruta graveolens*	rose	basil, cabbage, sage
Sage *Salvia officinalis*	cabbage, carrot, marjoram, strawberry, tomato	cucumber, rue
Savory *Satureja*	bean, onion	
Tansy *Tanacetum vulgare*	blackberry, pepper, potato, raspberry	
Tarragon *Artemisia dracunculus*	plants in general	
Thyme *Thymus*	cabbage, plants in general	
Yarrow *Achillea*	plants in general	

*Chive (*Allium schoenoprasum*) is a very versatile herb, both in
the kitchen and in the garden. It is reputed to be good friends
with carrots, grapes, parsley, and tomatoes. It is also quite lovely
to look at, especially when in flower, and can be used in the front
of the flower border.*

FRUIT AND THEIR COMPANIONS

A s with other plants in the garden there are benefits to be had by carefully mixing fruit crops with other plants. Below are listed those that are claimed to be good companions to fruit.

Also listed are other fruit and vegetables which are said to have a negative effect when grown close to certain fruit crops.

Fruit	Good companions	Poor companions
Apple *Malus pumila*	chive, nasturtium	potato
Blackberry *Rubus*	grape, tansy	
Citrus fruit *Citrus*	coffee, pepper	
Fig *Ficus carica*		rue
Grape *Vitus vinifera*	blackberry, hyssop, legume	cabbage, radish
Mulberry *Morus nigra*	grape	
Nectarine *Prunus persica*	asparagus, corn, grape, onion, strawberry	
Peach *Prunus persica*	asparagus, corn, grape, onion, strawberry	old and new peach trees
Pear *Pyrus communis*	currant	
Quince *Cydonia oblonga*	garlic	
Raspberry *Rubus idaeus*	tansy	blackberry, potato
Strawberry *Fragaria*	bean, borage, lettuce, nectarine, peach, spinach	cabbage, cauliflower, broccoli, Brussels sprout

MIX APPLE VARIETIES
FOR CROSS POLLINATION

Apple trees are not self-pollinating and must have a compatible tree of another variety planted nearby. When selecting varieties be certain to get at least two for each blossoming period to ensure a good pollination.

Early-blossoming apples	Mid-season-blossoming apples	Late-blossoming apples
Carroll	Earliblaze	Cortland
Jerseymae	Jonamac	Delicious
Julyred	McIntosh	Golden Delicious
Quinte	Niagra	Red Rome
Tydeman Early	Paulared	Rhode Island Greening
Viking	Prima	Stayman

Fruit trees can grow quite happily in most gardens. Vegetables and flowers can be planted right up to their trunks so long as the trees do not cast too much shade. Potatoes seem to be the one vegetable that doesn't grow well with fruit trees. Nasturtiums (Tropaeolum majus) and onions, on the other hand, are considered to be beneficial companions to them.

CHAPTER THREE

FLOWERS AND FOLIAGE

Plant compatibility, although the most important, is not the
only consideration when planning a companion garden.
Color, shape, texture, and even fragrance should all be taken
into account to provide interest throughout the year. Note the
successful use of sympathetic colors and contrasting shapes
in this garden (*left*).

NOTES ON COLOR

"I am strongly of the opinion that the possession of a quantity of plants, however good the plants may be themselves and however ample their number, does not make a garden; it only makes a *collection*. Having got the plants, the great thing is to use them with careful selection and definite intention." GERTRUDE JEKYLL

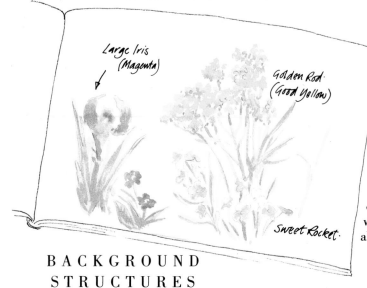

COLOR IDEAS

When visiting other gardens always carry a notebook and jot down ideas as you see them. Sketches or just lists of plants can be very useful when planning your own garden. Visit the same gardens at different times of the year and see how the plantings are affected by the changes of season. The act of writing or sketching will not only act as an *aide-mémoire* but will also make you look closer at the subject.

BACKGROUND STRUCTURES

When considering the color planting of your flower garden, remember it is not only the flowers and foliage that must be taken into account. The color of background walls, either of a building or a boundary wall, cannot be ignored and will often dictate the kind of planting that can be placed in front of it. If the color of the wall is objectionable for some reason, then consider covering it with a dense climber, such as ivy, to make it more suitable.

INCREASING PLANTS

Many herbaceous plants are large enough when purchased to be divided into two or more plants. These can be grown to give plenty of material for planting out. Growing the plants in a reserve bed allows you to check the colors before planting. Prepare the bed thoroughly and be certain that it is free of weeds, perennial ones in particular. In spring mark out on the soil a life-size outline of your plan and put in the plants. It is inevitable that some colors are going to be in the wrong place, so be prepared to move things around or even to obtain more suitable plants.

MIXING COLORS

A flower border would look very stiff and formal if each individual group of plants was kept distinct. Bedding plants, arranged in blocks or geometrical patterns, give this impression. Allow the different plants to fuse together so that the colors merge. Many plants, the violas and geraniums for example, will scramble through their neighbors, blurring the edges of their patches of color. This gives the border a more tranquil and natural appearance. The combination of two adjacent colors will not only make the transition more acceptable, it will also give the impression of another color.

Alchemilla mollis

Euphorbia

GREEN FLOWERS

Green is not normally considered a flower color, but there are a number of plants that have this curious property. It is fun in any garden to collect together a few curiosities and green flowers are certainly a good topic for conversation. Here are a few to try:

Aquilegia *Aquilegia viridiflora*
Bells of Ireland *Molucella laevis*
Corsican hellebore *Helleborus argutifolius*
Green hellebore *Helleborus viridiflorus*
Lady's mantle *Alchemilla mollis*
Lily *Lilium* 'Limelight'
Red hot poker *Kniphofia galpinii* 'Green Jade'
Spurge *Euphorbia*
Stinking hellebore *Helleborus foetidus*
Summer hyacinth *Galtonia viridiflora*
Tobacco plant *Nicotiana alata* 'Lime Green'

Helleborus foetidus

Helleborus argutifolius

COLOR HARMONY

So far in this book we have considered how plants relate to one another in practical ways, for reasons which benefit their well-being. But people are visual animals, and aesthetics play a great part in our lives. A jumble of plants is not a garden; some form of visual arrangement must be made in which color, shape, form, texture, even fragrance should all be taken into consideration.

Many gardeners wince at the thought of consciously attempting to make color relationships in the garden but think nothing of carefully choosing the colors of their clothes and home furnishings. What should make gardeners wince is not the thought of deliberately choosing colors for the garden, but rather the sheer variety of color at their disposal. In the United States there are many thousands of different perennial plants that can be purchased commercially, plus thousands more that are grown and distributed among friends and specialist societies. And that does not include the huge range of annuals available. Each of these plants is likely to have its own individual color, and, what is more, that color is likely to change as the flower ages and as the sun that shines on the garden changes its position throughout the day.

All these things give gardeners a tremendously large palette of colors to work with when designing gardens. It is also likely to give them problems, because unless the color relationships are carefully worked out, plants could clash or the overall effect could be spotty.

Shape and texture will be looked at later in the book, but at this point it should be mentioned that color should not be regarded in isolation. Rather, consider it in

This border is planted closely together in the cottage garden manner so that the plants support each other and suppress weeds. A tranquil effect is achieved by the blending of soft pink flowers and silver foliage.

Not all plantings are designed to provide tranquillity. Here a combination of the strong colors of the primroses (Primula) and the contrasting shapes of the primroses, Hosta, and the surrounding plants draw the eye to this point of interest. Such planting shows that the gardener has a very good grasp of how plants relate to each other visually.

relation to the overall design and layout of the garden. The background planting of trees, shrubs, and hedges, or structures such as walls and fences are important. The areas of sunlight and shade also have great effect on the color.

Certainly it is easier to put color into a garden if there is a framework of greenery into which it can be placed. A garden full of color and nothing else will look too brash and overpowering; it certainly will not have a tranquil effect. Greenery can be used to separate contrasting colors and to act as a break between different parts of the design. Some colors, particularly the paler ones, are shown off better against a green background.

One of the basic considerations when using color for any purpose is the question of contrast and harmony. The spectral colors can be arranged in a circle (known as a color wheel). Opposite colors on the wheel are known as complementary colors: red and green, yellow and violet, and blue and orange are examples. If these are placed next to each other the eye has to rapidly adjust and the result is a sense of restlessness. Adjacent colors on the wheel are much more harmonious to each other. They share certain pigments and blend together more easily.

The implications of this to gardeners are enormous. If plants with flowers of complementary colors are planted together, they will decidedly stand out from one another. The sudden change almost seems like a period in a sentence. If these color patterns are repeated down a border, the result is quite disturbing to the eye, as it keeps readjusting from one color to the other. This makes the border appear very restless.

On the other hand, flowers with colors adjacent to each other on the wheel blend in well together, allowing the eye to make a natural transition from one to the next. This is why it is recommended that the gentle transitions of adjacent colors be used as the foundation of the border, with complementary colors acting as focal points or sudden points of interest to stop the viewer here and there.

Another important aspect of color to remember is that some colors are considered warm and others cool. The reds, yellows, and oranges are the warm colors and the blues, grays, and violets the cool ones. Some of the warm colors are positively hot. These work particularly well in the bright light of hotter climates, but in the duller light of the North they have to be handled with care, otherwise they can become garish. The cool colors lose their impact in the brighter light of southern gardens but come into their own in duller, more

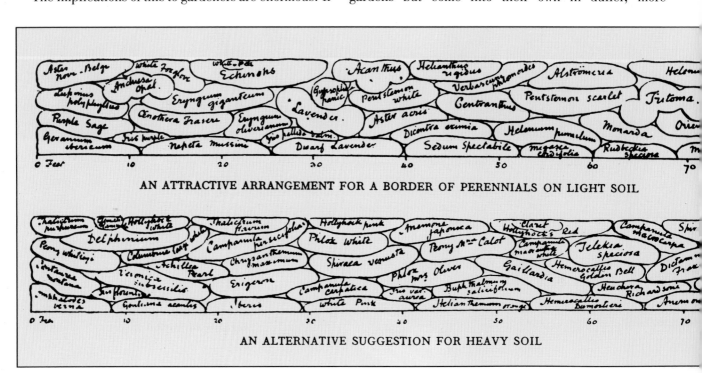

AN ATTRACTIVE ARRANGEMENT FOR A BORDER OF PERENNIALS ON LIGHT SOIL

AN ALTERNATIVE SUGGESTION FOR HEAVY SOIL

northerly light.

The warm colors engender a sense of excitement to a border; by contrast the cooler colors tend to give a feeling of tranquillity and peace. Both these feelings can be capitalized upon when drawing up the color scheme for the garden. Warm colors advance and cool ones recede. If pale blue or gray flowers are planted at the end of a border, the border will appear to be longer than it actually is. Conversely, one planted with hot reds or oranges will advance and seem shorter.

The use of color must inevitably become a question of trial and error. There are very few, if any, gardeners who can carry around in their heads the precise color of all the plants they are likely to use. When the plants flower there are bound to be those that need moving because the colors do not quite go together and they will sit more happily elsewhere in the border.

Even those gardeners who can remember the colors of each and every flower know that in the actual garden there is no such thing as a precise color. The latitude of the garden, the time of day, and the soil type will all effect the appearance of a color. Moreover, the color of one plant will be effected by the color of its neighbor. A dull color is likely to enliven a brighter one, for example.

This can all begin to get very technical and bewildering, but there are thousands of beautiful gardens out there which are either deliberately or accidentally following the basic rules of color. Look at other gardens, see where and why they are successful. At home draw out plans and color schemes on paper, then follow these plans in the border. Chances are your plans will need revisions of some kind, but then that is what learning is all about.

This is a good example of contrasting colors from opposite sides of the color wheel and contrasting shapes and forms of the globular and pendant flowers.

DRIFTS OF COLOR

Gertrude Jekyll, the revered English gardener and writer, popularized the use of drifts of color in the herbaceous border. She loved to build up color toward the center of the border with flowers of the strongest colors. She let these slowly diminish on each side of center right to the palest colors at the ends, leading the eye through a natural progression of a wide range of colors. In her writings she describes one such border: It starts with gray foliage. Then the flowers begin – pure blues at first, then ones of gray-blue, white, palest yellow, and palest pink, on through the stronger yellows to orange and finally red at the center. Then the border starts to recede by moving to orange, deep yellow to pale yellow, white and palest pink, and finally to purples and lilacs and the gray foliage at the end again.

THE COLOR WHEEL

Colors on a color wheel sympathetically merge into one another as they pass around the circle. Colors that lie opposite each other are contrasting and should be used in adjacent positions with care.

HOT COLORS

Hot colors include the bright reds, through scarlet to orangey red, on to orange, and finally to orangey yellow. These bright colors should be used sparingly, as the eye will tire of them quickly. They can be used where the mood needs enlivening or where emphasis is needed. Use them in bright sunlight, not in shade where their colors will be muted. A tracery of sunlight on them can be effective.

(Suggestions for hot-colored flowers are listed here because they are more difficult to find than cool-colored ones. Here and in the flower lists that follow only Latin names are generally given. This is because the common names of flowers, when they exist at all, tend to be very general and can vary greatly from one region to another. Where only the genus is given, as in the lists here, there are several species or hybrids that apply.)

Red flowers	Orange flowers	Yellow flowers
Antirrhinum	*Antirrhinum*	*Achillea*
Astilbe	*Anthemis*	*Alyssum saxatile*
Canna	*Campsis radicans*	*Anthemis*
Chaenomeles	*Canna*	*Antirrhinum*
Cheiranthus	*Cheiranthus*	*Calceolaria*
Crocosmia	*Calendula*	*Calendula*
Curtonus	*Crocosmia*	*Canna*
Dahlia	*Curtonus*	*Cestrum aurantiacum*
Desfontainea	*Dahlia*	*Cheiranthus*
Eccremocarpus scaber	*Eschscholzia*	*Coreopsis verticillata*
Embothrium coccineum	*californicum*	*Crocosmia*
Fuchsia	*Euphorbia griffithii*	*Dahlia*
Geum	'Dixter' and 'Fireglow'	*Eschscholzia*
Helianthemum	*Fritillaria imperialis*	*californicum*
Impatiens	*Gazania*	*Fremontodendron*
Lobelia cardinalis	*Helianthemum*	*californicum*
Lonicera × *brownii*	*Hemerocallis*	*Genista cinerea*
Lychnis chalcedonica	*Impatiens*	*Geum*
Monarda didyma	*Kniphofia*	*Helenium*
Paeonia	*Ligularia*	*Helianthus*
Papaver	*Lilium*	*Hemerocallis*
Pelargonium	*Papaver*	*Inula*
Penstemon	*Potentilla fruticosa*	*Kniphofia*
Phlox	'Red Ace' and	*Ligularia*
Potentilla (herbaceous)	'Tangerine'	*Primula*
Rhododendron (Azalea)	*Primula*	*Rhododendron* (Azalea)
Rosa	*Rhododendron* (Azalea)	*Rudbeckia*
Salvia	*Rosa*	*Rosa*
Tropaeolum	*Tagetes*	*Tagetes*
Tulipa	*Tropaeolum*	*Tropaeolum*
Zauschneria californica	*Tulipa*	*Tulipa*

The hot colors of the marigold (Tagetes) *'Butterscotch' would blend in with other similar colors such as the* Capsicum *(above). They could also be used as strong contrast by placing them next to blue flowers.*

The yellow of the Zinnia *'Gold Sun'* blends well
with the orange of the pods of the Capsicum
but would contrast rather badly with the pink
of the tulips (Tulipa) (opposite).

If strong, blue can be a startling color or, if
pale, soft and quiet. Blue is a difficult color,
as one of its partners is green, which is a
foliage rather than flower color. Its opposite
color is orange, with which it can form some
very vivid contrasts.

Mauve sits next to pink on the wheel and is
happiest with it in the garden. A startling
contrast can be made by planting some bright
yellow from the opposite side of the wheel
with it.

Pinks are always difficult colors to match;
they tend to go best with mauves and other
pastels. They impart an air of softness to a
border and are seen in their greatest contrast,
as here, against green.

FOLIAGE COLOR

Flowers are not the only providers of color in the garden; foliage also contributes a great deal of color. In a garden context green is not usually considered a color, but it has a great influence on what we see. The number of different greens that make up the overall impression is staggering. In particular, the spring produces a great variety of fresh greens. These tone down to a mid-green in the summer and by fall they are quite dull before they take on the colored tints and drop. Even evergreens change with the seasons. The liveliness of the new evergreen growth is partly due to the shiny surface of the leaves, which reflects the light, and partly due to the emerging leaves being paler as they have not taken up their complete fill of chlorophyll.

Green should certainly not be ignored as a color. It acts particularly as a foil for other colors and can create barriers between colors that would otherwise clash. A

Here is a wonderful contrast in foliage color from a group of Acer. As dramatic as they are, such contrasts should not be repeated too often because they can become visually uncomfortable and tiring on the eye.

Golden evergreen foliage provides a splash of color even on the dullest of winter's days, giving the impression of perpetual sunshine. Care must be taken in blending them.

enliven a border. They have a tendency to intensify the hot colors of flowers and act as a good background to many other colors, especially the pale ones. Most purple-leaved plants appreciate a sunny position.

Red is also a color of fall, and many green-leaved plants put on a brilliant red show just before they drop their leaves. Such shows are usually so powerful that they stand in their own right. Some woodland gardens are specifically planted for this time of year with drifts of colors: reds, bronze, golds, and yellows. Again drifts look better than a dotted arrangement, although the

Here is a fine combination of silver and purple foliage which is echoed by the flowers on the wall. Companion planting of this nature gives great pleasure.

garden without green is a very restless garden; green helps to calm the eye.

There are other foliage colors besides green. Silver foliage and gray foliage are quite common. These in many ways have the same effect in gardens as green does in calming down the fussiness of too much color. They are particularly useful for cooling down hot colors, and they are equally at home as a foil for the softer pinks and blues. Gray and silver are recessive colors and if planted at the end of a border will make it seem further away. Very few gray- or silver-leaved plants will tolerate shade, so they are best as plants of the open border.

Some plants have foliage that is almost red or purple, but a close examination will show that there is an element of green in the leaves as well. Many plants that have red leaves are at their brightest in the spring when their leaf chlorophyll (which is responsible for the green color in them) is still building up. If planted in a position where the sun can shine through the leaves, the foliage will often glow with a wonderful brilliance.

A garden planted entirely with red or purple foliaged plants would be very heavy and surprisingly dull, especially where it is not a natural foliage color. These warm colors are best used as contrasts to greens or used as accents. In small quantities they can be used to occasional accent tree with a particularly strong color does not go amiss.

Yellow or gold foliage plants add a lightness to a garden. As with red foliage, it would be wrong to plant the whole garden with these colors, but used with discretion they are marvelous at illuminating a dark corner. They look especially good against dark backgrounds such as conifers. In turn yellow or gold foliage is difficult to use as background for other plants. Unfortunately, nearly all yellow-foliaged plants scorch badly in the sun, so they really need some shade, especially from the strong midday sun. But since they look best brightening up a shady position, this is no real hardship.

Variegated-leaved plants are undergoing a vogue at the moment. These are plants whose leaves have patches, stripes, or spots of color different from the usual base one of green. The extra color can be silver, yellow, or purple. Sometimes, for example in *Houttuynia cordata* 'Chameleon' or *Salvia officinalis* 'Tricolor', there is more than one other color present.

For all their attraction variegated plants are difficult to relate to other plants. Again, they are good for

PURPLE-LEAVED PLANTS

Purple-leaved plants are increasing in popularity. They can be used to dramatic effect in a border but should never be overdone, because the border or garden will take on a dull, flat appearance.

Ajuga reptans 'Atropurpurea' and 'Burgundy Glow'
Canna 'Le Roi Humbert'
Clematis recta 'Purpurea'
Corylus maxima 'Purpurea'
Cotinus coggygria
Dahlia 'Bishop of Llandaff'
Lobelia cardinalis
Heuchera micrantha 'Palace Purple'
Ligularia dentata 'Desdemona' and 'Othello'
Phormium tenax
Ricinus communis
Rosa glauca
Rodgersia
Sambucus nigra 'Purpurea'
Weigela florida 'Foliis Purpureis'
Vitis vinifera 'Purpurea'

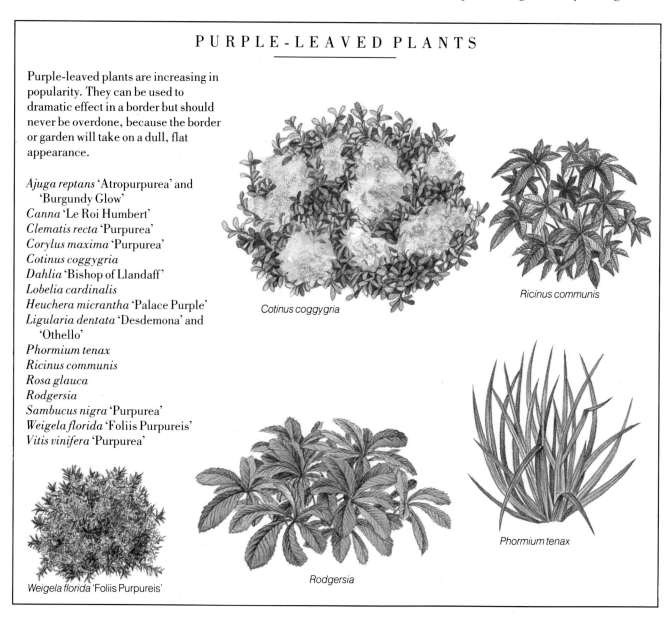

Cotinus coggygria

Ricinus communis

Weigela florida 'Foliis Purpureis'

Rodgersia

Phormium tenax

lightening up a dull spot or a mass of greenery. They are especially good on rainy, dull days when they give the garden a touch of artificial sunlight. The brightest variegations occur if the plant is in full sun, and unlike their all-yellow relations, they do not generally suffer sun scorch.

LEFT *Hosta is the most companionable of plants; it seems to fit into any planting design. The shape and texture of its leaves always adds interest to a border, as does its color. The variegated ones always help to brighten a dull corner.*

VARIEGATED-LEAVED PLANTS

Variegated-leaved plants add a bright touch to a border, particularly in the winter. Care should be taken not to place too many together, and color clashes should be avoided.

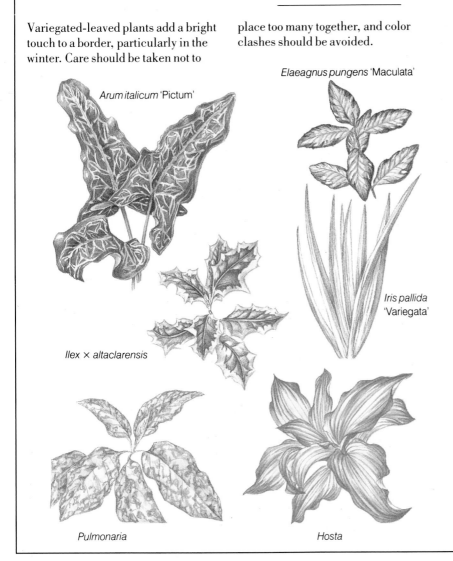

Arum italicum 'Pictum'

Elaeagnus pungens 'Maculata'

Iris pallida 'Variegata'

Ilex × *altaclarensis*

Pulmonaria

Hosta

Acer platanoides 'Drummondii'
Acorus calamnus 'Variegatus'
Arum italicum 'Pictum'
Brunnera macrophylla 'Hapsden Cream'
Convallaria majalis 'Variegata'
Cornus alba 'Elegantissima'
Cornus controversa 'Variegata'
Cyclamen hederifolium
Eleagnus pungens 'Maculata'
Euonymus fortunei 'Variegatus'
Fatsia japonica 'Variegata'
Fuchsia magellanica 'Variegata' and 'Versicolor'
Hedera colchica 'Dentata Variegata'
Hedera helix 'Buttercup' and 'Goldheart'
Hosta
Ilex × *altaclarensis* 'Golden King'
Iris pallida 'Variegata'
Kerria japonica 'Variegata'
Miscanthus sacchariflorus 'Zebrinus'
Osmanthus heterophyllus 'Variegatus'
Phlaris arundinacea 'Tricolor' and 'Variegata'
Phlox paniculata 'Nora Leigh'
Pieris japonica 'Variegata'
Phormium tenax 'Variegatum'
Pulmonaria
Sambucus nigra 'Marginata'
Symphytum grandiflorum 'Variegatum'
Sisyrinchium striatum 'Aunt May'

SINGLE COLOR SCHEMES

Many gardeners have been inspired by the well-known English gardens at Sissinghurst in Kent and at Hidcote Manor in Gloucestershire to produce gardens of a single color. Calling them single color gardens is not quite accurate, for while the basic flower color is restricted to one color, the foliage adds another dimension, rather like one-color printing in which the color of the paper must also be taken into account. Thus, the red borders at Hidcote Manor have red flowering plants backed with green and purple foliage, and at Sissinghurst the famous white garden contains flowers of that color along with green, gray, and silver foliage.

Making an entire garden or even a border of a single color is not an easy task. To keep the garden interesting a great deal of care must be given to the shapes and textures of the plants. Grading the colors is critical, too. It is surprising, for example, how many different shades of white there are and what difficulty there is in arranging them in a pleasing manner. In a white garden, flowers with a touch of green (a cool color) can work in well, but those that might have a bit of pink (a warm color) in them must definitely be left outside the garden gate. White is essentially a cold color, and any hint of a warm one will disturb the scheme.

It is often a good idea to relieve what can become a monotony of one color by adding touches of another color to it. This can be done dramatically, by, for instance, using *Lobelia cardinalis* as an accent in a white garden, where it would look like a slash of blood, or it can be more subtle, as at Sissinghurst, where silver foliage adds a gentler effect. In the Red Borders at Hidcote Manor orangey yellow in the form of *Hemerocallis* has been planted to act as punctuation throughout the borders.

Gardens of one color, particularly the pale or cool colors, tend to be very restful. Two colors tend to be more lively, and a mixture of white and yellow, for example, can be quite thrilling, particularly if reflecting water is involved.

A true monochrome garden can be created entirely out of green foliage. These can look most effective around modern buildings, perhaps with one dash of color. Ivy can be used to great effect in such gardens, scrambling over the ground as well as up and over structures.

The size of such single color schemes can vary from a whole garden, to one border or just an odd corner. In the case of a border or a corner, foliage in the form of shrubs or a hedge can divide the single color scheme from other plantings.

Red is always a difficult color to place in a garden. Creating a whole border devoted to this color presents a real challenge. But when the relationship between the plants works, as here, there is cause for great satisfaction.

WHITE FLOWERS

Below are listed a broad selection of white flowers ranging from the creamy white of the magnolias to the bright white of some of the *Dianthus* family.

Achillea ptarmica 'The Pearl'
Aconitum napellus 'Album'
Agapanthus campanulatus albus
Amelanchier
Anemone × hybridum 'Honorine Jobert'
Anemone nemorosa
Anthemis cupaniana
Anthericum liliago
Antirrhinum majus
Aquilegia vulgaris alba
Arabis
Aruncus dioicus
Aster
Astilbe rivularis
Bellis
Bergenia 'Silberlicht'
Campanula
Centranthus ruber albus
Cerastium tomentosum
Cimifuga cordifolia
Cistus
Choisya ternata
Chrysanthemum
Clematis
Convallaria majalis
Convolvulus cneorum
Crambe cordifolia
Dianthus
Dicentra
Digitalis purpurea 'Alba'
Epilobium angustifolium album
Erica herbacea 'Springwood White'
Escallonia 'Iveyi'
Eucryphia
Fritillaria meleagris alba
Galanthus
Galium odoratum

Geranium
Gladiolus
Gypsophila
Hebe
Heracleum mantegazzianum
Hesperis matrionalis
Hosta
Houttuynia cordata
Hydrangea
Iberis sempervirens
Iris
Jasminum
Lathyrus
Leucojum
Lilium
Lonicera fragrantissima
Lupinus
Lychnis coronaria 'Alba'
Lysimachia ephemerum
Magnolia

Malva moschata alba
Myrrhus odorata
Olearia
Omphalodes linifolia
Ornithogalum
Osmanthus delavayi
Osteospermum ecklonis
Paeonia
Petunia
Philadelphus
Phlox
Podophyllum
Polemonium
Polygonatum × hybridum
Potentilla fruticosa
Prunus
Pyrus
Rhododendron
Rodgersia
Romneya coulteri

White gardens are the most popular of those devoted to a single color. Gray and green foliage are used as foils.

Rosa
Sanguinaria canadensis
Saxifraga
Silene maritima
Smilacina racemosa
Spiraea
Syringa vulgaris 'Albus'
Thalictrum
Trillium grandiflorum
Tulipa
Verbascum
Veronica
Viola odorata alba
Viola septentrionalis
Zantedeschia aethiopica

NOTES ON SHAPE AND TEXTURE

So often color is thought of as being the main contributor to the appearance of a garden, but shape and texture play an equally important role.

FERNS

Ferns were extremely popular in Victorian times and interest in them is picking up. They are valuable because they provide a unique range of shapes and textures in among other plants or as background for them. They are also important in helping to keep the entire garden soil covered because many of them will grow in areas which other plants shun, namely dry and damp shade. Seen left, the shape and freshness of the new season's ferns make a contrasting foil to the colorful *Rhododendron*. Genera to try include:

Adiantum
Asplenium
Athyrium
Blechnum
Dryopteris
Matteuccia
Osmunda
Polypodium
Polystichium

Robinia pseudoacacia

Acer

Stachys byzantina

THE TALL AND THE THIN

There is a constant fascination in trees and shrubs that are fastigiate, or tall and columnar in shape, typified by the Mediterranean cypress *(Cupressus sempervirens)* or the Lombardy popular *(Populus nigra* 'Italica'). They can be very effective either rising out of other plants or as features in their own right on the horizon. Care must be taken not to use the shape too often or the garden will become restless to the eye. Some examples of plants that can be used include:

Acer platanoides 'Columnare'
Berberis thunbergii 'Erecta'
Betula pendula 'Fastigiata'
Carpinus betulus 'Columnaris'
Chamaecyparis lawsoniana 'Ellwoodii'

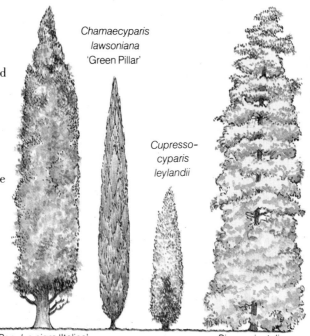

Chamaecyparis lawsoniana 'Green Pillar'

Cupresso-cyparis leylandii

Populus nigra 'Italica'

Picea orientalis

Crataegus monogyna 'Stricta'
Cupressus sempervirens
Juniperus chinensis 'Aurea'
Juniperus communis 'Compressa'
Juniperus communis 'Hibernica'
Juniperus virginiana 'Skyrocket'
Liriodendron tulipifera 'Fastigiata'
Populus nigra 'Italica'
Populus simonii 'Fastigiata'
Quercus petraea 'Columnaris'
Robinia pseudacacia 'Pyramidalis'
Taxus baccata 'Fastigiata'

TOPIARY

Trachycarpus fortunei

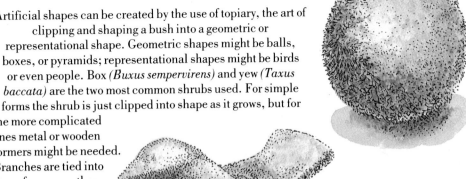

Artificial shapes can be created by the use of topiary, the art of clipping and shaping a bush into a geometric or representational shape. Geometric shapes might be balls, boxes, or pyramids; representational shapes might be birds or even people. Box *(Buxus sempervirens)* and yew *(Taxus baccata)* are the two most common shrubs used. For simple forms the shrub is just clipped into shape as it grows, but for the more complicated ones metal or wooden formers might be needed. Branches are tied into these formers as they develop. Large shapes may take many years to grow. Quicker ones can be created from privet *(Ligustrum ovalifolium)*, In a cottage garden setting the formality of the tightly clipped shrub contrasts well with the rest of the garden's informality.

Melianthus major

Mahonia

WATER

A water garden can be one of the loveliest and most effective types of companion plantings, for it provides a great opportunity for marrying together a large number of shapes and textures. On the water itself float the flat shapes of water lilies (*Nymphaea*). Standing in the water around its margins are the swordlike shapes of *Iris* and reeds. In the mud and on wet banks grow plants with a similar linear appearance, along with plants with a luscious growth of large, rounded leaves such as *Hosta* and *Ligularia*. Some of these, *Rheum* and *Gunnera* for example, take on gigantic proportions. Grasses and bamboos add visually to the scene and create a soothing constant rustling sound. All this is reflected in the water, giving motion to the shapes. Seen left, a jumble of shapes and textures of waterside plants almost obscuring the stream along which they grow.

SHAPE AND TEXTURE OF PLANTS

Flower color alone is not what gives a garden its attractive appearance. Consideration must also be given to how the shapes and textures of the plants relate to one another.

As a basic shape the hedge surrounding the garden gives an enclosing feeling, defining the limit of the garden and providing the background against which many of the plants will be seen. It also sets the tone of the garden. If clipped it gives a formal appearance; if unclipped it can give a background air of informality. Some informal hedging shrubs, such as *Berberis*, need to be left unclipped if they are to flower.

Trees and shrubs are the other background forms. The general shapes of such plants usually do little more than provide a backdrop. Occasionally they should be planted to give extra emphasis. Tall, columnar plants give an obvious vertical stress, climbing plants will also lead the eye upward and out of the garden. It is obvious that these vertical plants should be behind other plants. Conversely, the low-growing carpeting shrubs, and herbaceous material for that matter, tend to keep the eye creeping over the ground and therefore should be planted toward the front of borders and on the edges of paths.

*A contrast in shape and texture is found here, as the flat, round leaves of the nasturtium (*Tropaeolum majus*) float above the glaucous cut leaves of the rue (*Ruta graveolens*).*

LEFT *A young dogwood* (Cornus controversa *'Variegata') is beginning to extend its flat horizontal branches against a background of dark evergreens. The contrast between the dogwood and its background is quite startling and shows what can be achieved with careful placing of plants. In this case the background is not only a foil, it also provides shelter.*

The carpeting effect of some plants, especially uniform ground cover, can be broken by other shapes. Rounded ones provide a gentle reminder that there are other things about, and more spiky ones, such as *Delphinium* and foxglove (*Digitalis purpurea*), produce a more startling vertical emphasis. A border that contains plants that are all of the same general shape can be extremely boring. Fortunately there are usually enough plants with different structural as well as foliage shapes to vary the overall appearance of a garden.

Trees, shrubs, or herbaceous plants with an arresting appearance can be used as focal points or almost as pieces of sculpture, either alone or incorporated in a border. Imagine the spires of a towering *Delphinium* pointing toward the sky, or the statuesque giant thistle (*Onopordum acanthium*) as it suddenly erupts out of an herbaceous border, or a solitary plant of *Cornus controversa* 'Variegata', with its silvery horizontal branches highlighted against a dark background of conifers.

Two plants can have a similar outline, but when other factors such as the shape and density of the leaves are taken into account, they can appear quite different. For example, the outline appearance of tamarisk (*Tamarix*) and some of the rhododendrons (*Rhododendron*) are very

ABOVE *The scotch thistle (*Onopordum acanthium*) is a very statuesque plant whose silver foliage and candelabra-like stems create a dramatic picture in the border.*

similar, but the effect of each is as different as chalk and cheese. Tamarisk has fine, feathery foliage and dainty feathery flowers, giving it a strong feeling of lightness and airiness; the rhododendron, on the other hand, has large, leathery leaves of a somber color and big, heavy trusses of flowers, giving it a very solid, fixed-to-the-earth feeling.

A plant's leaves usually last much longer than the flowers and consequently have a greater lasting effect on the garden's appearance. As with color, too much variation in the texture they provide can be disturbing, but likewise too little variation can become boring. A scene of unrelieved conifers is rather like having a carpet draped over the garden, which even varying the shape and color of the other plantings can do little to relieve. Putting in a carpet of heathers (*Erica*) around their skirts does not improve matters but tends rather to increase the boredom.

Some plants are terribly drab both in shape and foliage when they are out of flower. *Viburnum farreri*, for example, is valuable for its show of fragrant flowers during the winter. But for the rest of the year its gawky, stiff stems are best hidden by other plants, either by planting it toward the back of a bed where it will be lost among more interesting vegetation, or by growing a climber through it (*Clematis*, for instance) to give it more interest later in the year.

When you think about shape and texture don't just consider the leaves and overall plant; the shape of the flower spikes themselves are important. One has only got to think of the flat tops of *Achillea*, the round balls of *Allium*, the fat candles of *Astilbe*, or tall spires of *Delphinium* to appreciate the effect they can have on the appearance of the garden.

RIGHT *Viburnum* farreri *is very useful, as it blossoms in the flower-starved winter, but it is rather ugly for the rest of the year. Like similar plants, it needs companions to grow through it or in front of it when it is not in flower.*

LEFT *A section of a red border demonstrating the excitement of variations in shapes between the poppy (*Papaver bracteatum *'Goliath') and the spiky, straplike leaves of New Zealand flax (*Phormium tenuifolium*).*

THE SEASONS

All the seasons of the year have much to offer the gardener. Careful planting can extend the garden growing season well into the year, even into the heart of winter. And then there are many other garden-related jobs that need to be done even when the garden itself is idle.

GRASSES

Ornamental grasses, for good reason, are becoming popular, with their interesting shapes, enhanced by their movement and sound. They can contribute much to successional plantings because they retain their attractiveness even after their flowering season. As fall comes they go brown and sere and they will continue to stand through the winter, giving color, texture, and shape to the borders and providing seeds as winter fodder for birds and small mammals. Some are really statuesque, reaching several yards (meters) high. Large clumps can be used as focal points and can look particularly good when seen over water. They associate well with other plants.

WINTER GARDENS

Gardeners who have lots of space to spare may want to have separate winter gardens that show off the more subtle beauty of the quietest season of the year. Even more modest-sized gardens can look lovely in winter if they are carefully planted with some of the trees and shrubs that are particularly interesting then. Winter gardens might contain winter-flowering plants, such as *hellebores* or trees and shrubs with interesting bark, like some of the maples *(Acer)* or birches *(Betula)*. The lower winter sun will often enliven the red, black, and yellow barks of some of the willows *(Salix)*. Many of the winter-flowering shrubs are highly perfumed, and branches can be picked and brought into the house. Evergreen variegated plants are useful for brightening up a dull day, giving it a touch of artificial sunlight.

Even if there is not room for a complete winter garden, you should aim to grow at least a few plants and shrubs to provide interest at this time of year.

Acer campestre

Salix fragilis

Betula pendula

Cornus

SPRING BULBS

Spring is the time for bulbs. Tulips *(Tulipa)* and bluebells *(Hyacinthoides non-scripta)* flower among the expanding fronds of the lady fern *(Athyrium filix-femina)* (right). The fern will continue to grow, covering the unsightly, dying leaves of the bulbs.

DEADHEADING

During the summer months, when flowering is at its height, regular deadheading will not only help to keep the plants neat but will also help to promote repeat-flowering. Naturally if you want to keep some seed for sowing next year, allow a few of the heads to develop and go to seed.

THROUGH THE SEASONS

It is a good idea to take snapshots of your garden throughout the year. Knowing what the garden looks like in other seasons is important when it comes to adding new plants to a border. It is useful, for example, to know in spring (the main planting season) what the garden will look like in fall and how extra plants might affect it.

FALL LEAVES

It is a waste of a valuable natural resource to burn leaves. They should be stacked, preferably in a wire container to prevent them from blowing away, and left to decompose. Since they take longer to rot down than compost, expect it to be two years or more before they can be used.

SUCCESSIONAL PLANTING

At its simplest, successional planting in the flower garden means relating plants to each other so that there is a maximum of color and interest in the garden throughout the year.

In many of the larger gardens in former, grander times, it was not unusual to find successional planting of sorts achieved through a series of sub-gardens. These were individual gardens, each planted specifically to show off the flowers of one particular season. Sub-gardens would be visited·and admired in their due season and then ignored for the rest of the year. Although winter gardens can still sometimes be found, filled with winter-flowering plants or plants that have striking colored bark or evergreen foliage, seasonal gardens are now rare. That is because they are almost impossible to establish in anything but the largest gardens where space, time, and money are not limited.

In addition to being extravagant, such sub-gardens cannot take advantage of all the benefits of well-planned successional plantings. As in the vegetable garden, when compatible plants that mature at different times are grown together in one garden, the ground stays covered at all times of the year. This helps to control weeds, and it helps to keep the soil from drying out in dry weather and from eroding during heavy rains. It also allows you to grow and enjoy the maximum number of plants in a given garden space.

For effective successional planting lay out your flower borders in such a way that adjacent plants flower at different times of the year. For example, the neighbors to the winter-flowering hellebores (*Helleborus orientalis*) could be the bleeding heart (*Dicentra spectabilis*) for spring, *Penstemon*, for summer and *Aster novi-belgii* for fall. Depending on what varieties you choose, they could all be red or reddish purple or even white, giving a continuity of color in that part of the border. While hellebores are in flower, the others would be just emerging. Hellebores appreciate some shade from the hot summer's sun and the other plants would tower over them in turn, giving them the protection they need.

In that example, the plants would be grown next to one another. An even closer form of successional planting can be achieved by underplanting. Here bulbs are planted very close to herbaceous plants or under low shrubs. In the first instance daffodils (*Narcissus*) might be planted next to a *Geranium pratense*. The daffodil

ABOVE *A dark* Aubrieta *forms a wonderful background to these pink tulips (*Tulipa*). Later the ground will be taken over by completely different flowers.*

TOP *Early summer flowers replace the spring ones. The pink oriental poppies (*Papaver orientalis*) will in turn fade and die, and the hummock of dark green foliage will expand to produce blue geraniums in their place.*

RIGHT *This lightly shaded border is a veritable jungle of spring flowers. As the year progresses the image will drastically change; different plants will spring up to produce flowers that will replace those seen here.*

comes up and blooms, and as it dies back the shriveling foliage is covered by the geranium as its growth speeds up in the late spring. Snowdrops (*Galanthus*) can be used to grow through low-growing shrubs such as heather (*Erica*), which generally looks fairly dull when the snowdrop is in flower but comes into its own when the snowdrop dies back. Bulbs are not confined to spring. Lilies (*Lilium*) can be interplanted with herbaceous or shrubby plants, the summer bulb itself appreciating the cool situation provided by the foliage of other plants. Similarly, montbretia (*Crocosmia*), which

generally blooms in late summer, can be planted in between other plants.

Floppy plants can be of use later in the season to cover up holes left by other plants. For example, the oriental poppy (*Papaver orientalis*) looks a mess when the flowers are over. It can be cut to the ground and a clambering plant such as *Lathyrus latifolius* can be allowed to sprawl over its place.

Climbing plants can be used to provide color for trees or shrubs that have flowered earlier in the season. It is possible to run two or more climbers together, each

*This vertical garden brightens the front of a house with a
wonderful splash of color. By using pots and bringing in new
plants to replace those that fade, the display can be kept up all
through the summer. Great attention must be given to watering,
particularly the clay pots, which could need watering several
times a day during very hot spells.*

having a different flowering period. Climbers need not always climb, they can be allowed to scramble over a dull ground cover or even over herbaceous plants that have finished flowering, as mentioned above.

There are several other ways of filling gaps left by vegetation that has died back. One way is to plant annuals in its place. This involves preparation, since the annuals should be sown at the right time so that they will be mature and flowering when neighboring plants are spent. Another way is to actually move new plants into position. For example, many of the herbaceous plants with fibrous roots such as Michaelmas daisies

(*Aster novi-belgii*) can be moved when they are in full flower if they are given a good soaking prior to transplanting. The asters can be lined out in a spare piece of ground, perhaps at the back of a border. Water them several hours before moving and then dig them up, leaving good rootballs of soil on the plants. They can be moved into prepared holes and again watered. If done carefully the plants will not notice the move. You could also grow a number of plants in quite large pots. When required the pot can be plunged in the garden soil so that the soil covers the rim, giving the impression that the plant has been there all the time.

ABOVE *In the open meadows most of the flowers are over by the summer when the hay is cut, but even here flowers can be seen from early spring until midsummer.*

LEFT *Shady areas are more difficult to keep in flower throughout the year, but foliage alone can provide a great deal of interest.*

SPRING-FLOWERING PLANTS

Spring is the time when the garden is at its most exciting. It is the season when everything is fresh and new. Bright colors are shown off against the fresh greens of the new foliage, and the plants yet to flower act as perfect foils to the spring colors.

1 Japanese crimson glory vine *Vitis coignetiae*
2 Winter jasmine *Jasminum nudiflorum*
3 Japonica *Chaenomeles speciosa* 'Nivalis'
4 Smoke bush *Cotinus coggygria*
5 Hazel *Corylus avellana*
6 Hebe *Hebe albicans*
7 Witch hazel *Hamamelis mollis*
8 Rock rose *Helianthemum nummularium*
9 Cotoneaster *Cotoneaster*

10 Hawthorn *Crataegus crus-galli*
11 Flowering cherry *Prunus × subhirtella* 'Autumnalis'
12 Viburnum *Viburnum davidii*
13 Hypericum *Hypericum × moserianum*
14 Hellebore *Helleborus*
15 Hawthorn *Crataegus monogyna*
16 Winter honeysuckle *Lonicera fragrantissima*
17 Heuchera *Heuchera sanguinea*

18 Holly *Ilex aquifolium*
19 Daphne *Daphne odora*
20 Deutzia *Deutzia gracilis*
21 Rock rose *Cistus*
22 Yucca *Yucca*
23 Californian lilac *Ceanothus*
24 Mock orange *Philadelphus*
25 Periwinkle *Vinca minor*
26 Pink *Dianthus*
27 Crocus & scilla *Crocus & Scilla*
28 Tulip & muscari *Tulipa kaufmanniana & Muscari*

29 Daffodil *Narcissus* 'Irish Luck'
30 Crown imperial *Fritillaria imperialis*
31 Daffodil & windflower *Narcissus pseudonarcissus & Anemone blanda*
32 Primrose *Primula vulgaris*
33 Iris *Iris sibirica*
34 Clematis *Clematis viticella*
35 Clematis *Clematis montana*
36 Tulip & brunnera *Tulipa* 'Athleet' & *Brunnera macrophylla*

37 Windflower *Anemone blanda*
38 Geranium *Geranium endressii*
39 Tubs of hyacinth & daffodil *Hyacinthus & narcissus*

SUMMER-FLOWERING PLANTS

In summer the garden takes on a more settled look. The bright sun often drains away the color of the flowers and the foliage begins to dull a little. The bees add to the drowsy atmosphere. Good plant relationships are particularly important to cover the gaps of the spent spring flowers.

1 Japanese crimson glory vine *Vitis coignetiae*

2 Winter jasmine *Jasminum nudiflorum*

3 Japonica *Chaenomeles speciosa* 'Nivalis'

4 Smoke bush *Cotinus coggygria*

5 Hazel *Corylus avellana*

6 Hebe *Hebe albicans*

7 Witch hazel *Hamamelis mollis*

8 Rock rose *Helianthemum nummularium*

9 Cotoneaster *Cotoneaster*

10 Hawthorn *Crataegus crus-galli*

11 Flowering cherry *Prunus × subhirtella* 'Autumnalis'

12 Viburnum *Viburnum davidii*

13 Hypericum *Hypericum × moserianum*

14 Hellebore *Helleborus*

15 Hawthorn *Crataegus monogyna*

16 Winter honeysuckle *Lonicera fragrantissima*

17 Heuchera *Heuchera sanguinea*

18 Holly *Ilex aquifolium*

19 Daphne *Daphne odora*

20 Deutzia *Deutzia gracilis*

21 Rock rose *Cistus*

22 Yucca *Yucca*

23 Californian lilac *Ceanothus*

24 Mock orange *Philadelphus*

25 Periwinkle *Vinca minor*

26 Pink *Dianthus*

27 Brunnera *Brunnera macrophylla*

28 Turk's-cap lily *Lilium martagon*

29 Aster *Aster lateriflorus*

30 Dusty miller *Lychnis coronaria*

31 Ornamental onion *Allium cernuum*

32 Clematis *Clematis viticella*

33 Clematis *Clematis montana*

34 Iris *Iris sibirica*

35 Knotweed *Polygonum amplexicaule*

36 Hosta *Hosta*

37 Montbretia *Crocosmia*

38 Geranium *Geranium endressii*

39 Spurge *Euphorbia polychroma*

40 Day lily *Hemerocallis thunbergii*

41 Montbretia *Crocosmia* 'Solfaterre'

42 Dahlia *Dahlia* 'Bishop of Llandaff'

43 Euphorbia *Euphorbia griffithii*

44 Lily *Lilium pardalinum*

45 Hollyhock *Alcea rosea*

46 Red-hot poker *Kniphofia*

47 Rose *Rosa*

48 Tub of miniature roses, petunia & lobelia *Rosa, Petunia & Lobelia*

FALL PLANTS

Fall is a difficult time in the garden, as gaps begin to appear, left by the dying flowers of spring and summer. Foliage color and berries take on an important role. Contrast can be given to these and other warm fall colors by introducing the blues of various asters.

1 Japanese crimson glory vine *Vitis coignetiae*
2 Winter jasmine *Jasminum nudiflorum*
3 Japonica *Chaenomeles speciosa* 'Nivalis'
4 Smoke bush *Cotinus coggygria*
5 Hazel *Corylus avellana*
6 Hebe *Hebe albicans*
7 Witch hazel *Hamamelis mollis*
8 Rock rose *Helianthemum nummularium*
9 Cotoneaster *Cotoneaster*
10 Hawthorn *Crataegus crus-galli*
11 Flowering cherry *Prunus* × *subhirtella* 'Autumnalis'
12 Viburnum *Viburnum davidii*
13 Hypericum *Hypericum* × *moserianum*
14 Hellebore *Helleborus*
15 Hawthorn *Crataegus monogyna*
16 Winter honeysuckle *Lonicera fragrantissima*
17 Heuchera *Heuchera sanguinea*
18 Holly *Ilex aquifolium*
19 Daphne *Daphne odora*
20 Deutzia *Deutzia gracilis*
21 Rock rose *Cistus*
22 Yucca *Yucca*
23 Californian lilac *Ceanothus*
24 Mock orange *Philadelphus*
25 Periwinkle *Vinca minor*
26 Pink *Dianthus*
27 Brunnera *Brunnera macrophylla*
28 Kaffir lily *Schizostylis coccinea*
29 Aster *Aster lateriflorus* 'Horizontalis'
30 Dusty miller *Lychnis coronaria*
31 Ornamental onion *Allium cernuum*
32 Clematis *Clematis viticella*
33 Clematis *Clematis montana*
34 Iris *Iris sibirica*
35 Knotweed *Polygonum amplexicaule*
36 Hosta *Hosta*
37 Montbretia *Crocosmia*
38 Geranium *Geranium endressii*
39 Spurge *Euphorbia polychroma*
40 Day lily *Hemerocallis thunbergii*
41 Montbretia *Crocosmia* 'Solfaterre'
42 Dahlia *Dahlia* 'Bishop of Llandaff'
43 Euphorbia *Euphorbia griffithii*

WINTER PLANTS

Winter is expected to be bare in the garden so any plant in flower is a bonus. Evergreen foliage, the color of bark, and the shape of trees and shrubs can supplement the interest of the few flowers that brave the weather. Many winter flowers are fragrant, so plant where they can be smelled.

1 Japanese crimson glory vine *Vitis coignetiae*
2 Winter jasmine *Jasminum nudiflorum*
3 Japonica *Chaenomeles speciosa* 'Nivalis'
4 Smoke bush *Cotinus coggygria*
5 Hazel *Corylus avellana*
6 Hebe *Hebe albicans*
7 Witch hazel *Hamamelis mollis*

8 Rock rose *Helianthemum nummularium*
9 Cotoneaster *Cotoneaster*
10 Hawthorn *Crataegus crus-galli*
11 Flowering cherry *Prunus* × *subhirtella* 'Autumnalis'
12 Viburnum *Viburnum davidii*
13 Hypericum *Hypericum* × *moserianum*

14 Hellebore *Helleborus*
15 Hawthorn *Crataegus monogyna*
16 Winter honeysuckle *Lonicera fragrantissima*
17 Heuchera *Heuchera sanguinea*
18 Holly *Ilex aquifolium*
19 Daphne *Daphne odora*
20 Deutzia *Deutzia gracilis*
21 Rock rose *Cistus*

22 Yucca *Yucca*
23 Californian lilac *Ceanothu*
24 Mock orange *Philadelphus*
25 Periwinkle *Vinca minor*
26 Pink *Dianthus*

MUTUAL SUPPORT

Many plants, particularly climbing ones, need support of some kind. The most natural way of achieving this is to allow them to climb through other plants.

PLANTING CLIMBERS

When planting climbing plants next to walls, do not put them too close. The area against walls is nearly always very dry. Dig the hole at least 1½ft (45cm) out from the base and dig in plenty of moisture-retentive compost or manure.

Similarly never plant too close to the trunk of a tree for the same reason. If possible start climbing plants from outside the spread of the tree's canopy. This will ensure that the plant gets plenty of moisture.

COOL ROOTS

Many climbers, in particular *Clematis*, like to have hot heads but cool roots. The latter can easily be achieved by covering the root area with a few stones. Alternatively, a good thick mulch of manure helps. And so does using companion planting, by placing other plants nearby so that the sun does not penetrate to the base of the *Clematis*.

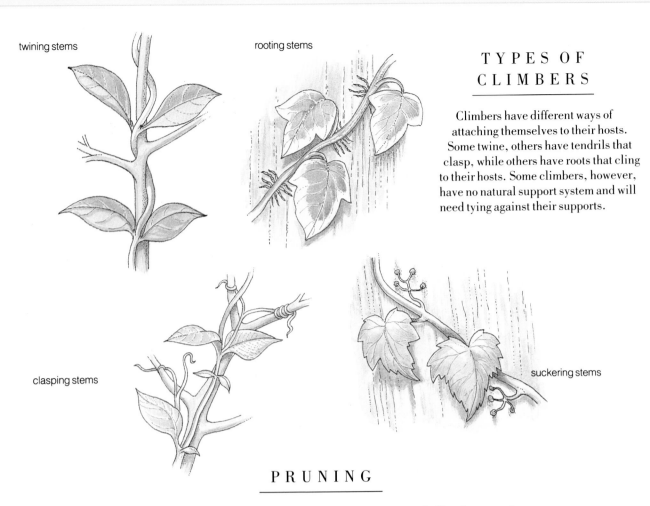

twining stems

rooting stems

clasping stems

suckering stems

TYPES OF CLIMBERS

Climbers have different ways of attaching themselves to their hosts. Some twine, others have tendrils that clasp, while others have roots that cling to their hosts. Some climbers, however, have no natural support system and will need tying against their supports.

PRUNING

It is very easy to overlook the pruning of climbers, and they can soon become a tangled mass of dead stems. Some, such as some *Clematis*, should be cut almost to the ground each year. Others only need to have the dead wood removed, while a third group needs to have some of its older wood pruned off each year so that the complete plant is renovated over three or four years. Check the times and amount of pruning that each plant requires and, if necessary, note this on a label and attach it permanently to the plant.

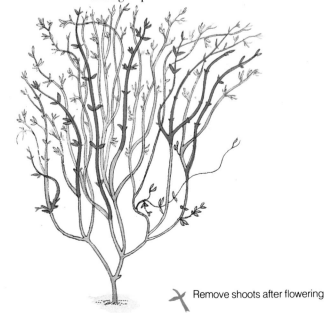

Remove shoots after flowering

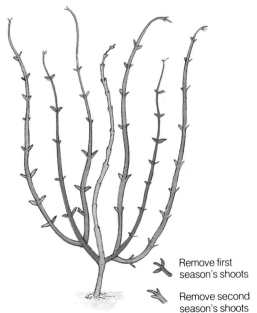

Remove first season's shoots

Remove second season's shoots

SUPPORTS FOR PLANTS

One of the most tedious jobs around a garden is preventing plants from being blown over in the wind. To a certain extent this can be achieved by providing wind breaks, as discussed on pages 28-29, but staking tall and climbing plants is often needed.

If the garden adheres to cottage garden principles, then plants will be planted so close together that they will all act as mutual supports. Careful planning is needed to ensure that the plants are graded in height. Obviously *Delphinium* will not be supported by *Aubrieta*, but if planted tightly next to other strong growing plants such as *Inula helenium*, it should be able to stay upright without other support.

If support is needed, vegetative material, such as peasticks, forms a more natural framework through which the plants can grow than will plastic or metal. To prepare such material sticks of hazel (*Corylus*) or other twiggy branches should be cut and stored before their leaves have been formed. When required, they are pushed into the ground and their tops bent over and tied together to form a rigid framework.

Climbers and scramblers almost always need support, even if wind is not a factor. These are often grown up walls or fences with the aid of wires or eyes fixed to the support. However, as in natural environments plants can support climbers and scramblers. A typical example would be old apple trees through which *Clematis* or roses (*Rosa*) are growing. The apple trees may be too old to produce apples, but they provide very nice support for the lovely *Clematis* and rose flowers.

A climber can be grown through another flowering shrub or tree, or two climbers can be grown together up a wall or over an arbor. The beauty of this is that if the climber and its living support, or, in the second case, the two climbers, are carefully selected, they will flower at different times, keeping that space in flower for a long time, perhaps even into the cold months if a winter-flowering shrub has been chosen.

The combinations are endless. *Clematis* is an obvious choice. This lovely climbing plant can be grown through other climbers such as roses or *Solanum* or through a multitude of shrubs. And annual climbers as well as perennial climbers can be used; nasturtium (*Tropaeolum majus*) and morning glory (*Ipomoea*) can be effective growing through a shrub.

*Plants can be supported by inserting hazel (*Corylus*) branches into the ground, bending them over, and interweaving their tips. This should be done while the plant is still small so that as it increases in size, it grows through the sticks. The result is that the sticks support the plant and, if the sticks are placed close enough to the base, the plant hides them.*

FLOWERING CLIMBING PLANTS

The precise flowering time will vary from place to place; although many plants listed here flower in the summer, they will do so at different times.

ABOVE *Old apple or other trees make excellent supports for climbing* Clematis, *particularly those such as* C. montana, *which need little pruning.*

Plant name	Flowering season
Akebia *Akebia quinata*	spring
Bomarea *Bomarea*	summer
Bougainvillea *Bougainvillea*	summer
Bukahara fleece flower *Polygonum baldschuanicum*	summer, fall
Campsis *Campsis grandiflora*	summer, fall
Chilean bell-flower *Lapageria rosea*	summer
Clematis *Clematis*	spring, summer
Clematis armandii	winter, spring
Clerodendron *Clerodendron thomsoniae*	summer
Cobaea *Cobaea scandens*	fall, winter
Eccremocarpus *Eccremocarpus scaber*	summer, fall
Holboellia *Holboellia coriacea*	spring
Honeysuckle *Lonicera*	summer
Hydrangea *Hydrangea petiolaris*	summer
Jasmine *Jasminum*	summer
Mandevilla *Mandevilla*	summer
Morning glory *Ipomoea*	summer
Nasturtium *Tropaeolum*	summer, fall
Passion flower *Passiflora*	summer
Pileostegia *Pileostegia viburnoides*	fall
Plumbago *Plumbago auriculata*	fall
Rhodochiton *Rhodochiton atrosanguineum*	summer, fall
Rose *Rosa*	summer
Solanum *Solanum crispum*	spring, summer
Solanum jasminoides	summer
Thunbergia *Thunbergia*	spring, summer
Winter honeysuckle *Lonicera fragrantissima*	winter
Winter jasmine *Jasminum nudiflorum*	winter

Wisteria *and honeysuckle* (Lonicera) *are growing through each other, giving a wonderful blend of colors and contrasts.*

Lapageria rosea *flowers through a* Pyracantha *which is in berry, providing another good contrast in color and shape.*

CHAPTER FOUR

THE INTEGRATED GARDEN

If one chooses carefully, vegetables, flowers, herbs, and fruit can all be grown quite happily together in one garden; they need not be separated off into individual sections. On the page opposite, herbs are grown in a flower border.

NOTES ON COMBINING FLOWERS AND VEGETABLES

Vegetables, herbs, and fruit are decorative as well as useful and blend well with flowering plants. The entire garden should be taken into consideration when deciding what should be included.

NECESSARY COMPANIONS

There are some plants, called dioecious, which have male and female flowers on separate plants. Well-known examples are holly (*Ilex*) and skimmia (*Skimmia*), which is shown on the left. In order for berries to be produced there must be both male and female plants within the immediate neighborhood, with bees ferrying the pollen between them. So when buying skimmia, for example, be careful to buy one of each sex, or you will not get the beautiful berries for which they are grown. If you do not want the seed, the male flower is more decorative, as in some of the New Zealand clematis or in some of the willows. Some dioecious plants include:

Antennaria *Antennaria dioica*
Butchers broom *Ruscus aculeatus*
Campion *Silene dioica*
Clematis *Clematis marmoraria*
     Clematis petriei
Holly *Ilex*
Pernettya *Pernettya*
Sea buckthorn *Hippophae rhamnoides*
Skimmia *Skimmia*
Willow *Salix*

GOING TO SEED

Apart from plants such as peas and beans where the seed is the part that is eaten, few vegetables are allowed to run to seed. However, there is no reason why a few should not be allowed to stay in the ground for another season to flower. Not only will they produce seed that can be collected and used for the next crop, but there will also be the decorative flower heads to enjoy – as in the case of radish, shown right. In addition, many of them, in particular the umbellifers such as carrots and parsnips, are very attractive to hoverflies and predatory wasps, both of which are useful for controlling insect pests.

ASPARAGUS

One of the most decorative of vegetables is asparagus. After midsummer the harvesting of the asparagus shoots is abandoned to allow the plants to build up reserves for the following year. The shoots develop into 5-6ft (1.5-1.8m) stems bearing very fine, ferny leaves. These are wonderfully decorative both in the garden and when cut for the house.

The young crowns should be planted in free-draining soil and supplied with ample farmyard manure. Cutting in the first year should be restricted to just a few shoots to allow the plant to develop.

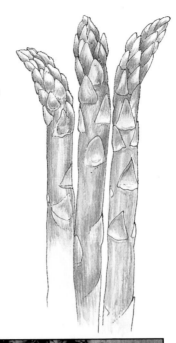

DECORATIVE FRUIT TREES

Most fruit trees can be trained in decorative fashions that add interest to both the vegetable and flower gardens (left). They can be trained up a wall or against wires, forming backgrounds or natural divisions within the garden. Espaliers or cordons are the most usual way of training them (below).

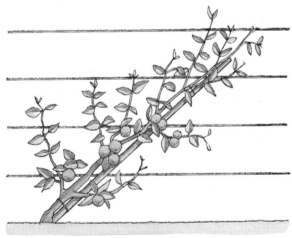

cordon

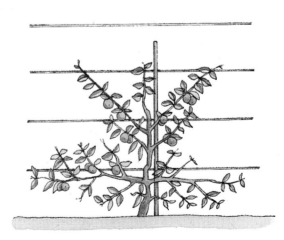

espalier

FLOWERS AND VEGETABLES TOGETHER

In their native environments flowers and vegetables do not grow separately, but together. Keeping them apart in the garden is unnatural. Be that as it may, gardeners of the past and of today generally keep flowers in the decorative garden and vegetables in the functional one, with the plants laid out in neat rows.

Many people like to see orderly vegetable plots, indeed, many like to see orderly flower beds as well, with bedding plants neatly lined up together to the nearest inch. However, gardening is not a geometric exercise; it is something both to give pleasure and to produce food. There is no reason why the two should not go together – in the same garden beds.

As we have already seen, quite a number of flowers are actually beneficial to neighboring vegetables. Flowering plants have regularly been planted in rows or intermingled with vegetable crops to help protect them

Summer squash and coneflower (Rudbeckia) growing decoratively together. Vegetables and flowers can be grown together for a host of reasons, but particularly to help each other repel pests and to make the garden visually more interesting.

from pestilent insects and in some cases in the belief that they help the crop grow or improve its flavor. This mixing of different types of plants in one bed makes not only for an attractive border with more color and textures, but increases the number of scents, and even adds to the overall atmosphere of the garden, with the additional evocative sounds of the bees and hoverflies. These aspects of a garden may seem trivial, but a garden is to be enjoyed as well as to be productive. Looking at the garden from a different aspect, a large number of vegetables work well in a flower border. In many of the old cottage gardens the two merged and there was no defined line. Runner beans grown up wigwams of poles or sticks give a very decorative background to any border. Many vegetables – ornamental cabbages or ruby chard for instance – are very colorful and look just as

ABOVE *French marigolds (Tagetes patula) and tomatoes are classic companions. The marigolds reduce the number of nematodes in the soil which could stunt the growth of tomatoes. They also attract hoverflies which prey on the bothersome aphid population.*

RIGHT *This bed shows how lovely flowers and vegetables can be when planted together. The vegetables here are decorative in their own right, but the flowering plants add to the pleasant visual effect.*

good in the flower border as they do in the vegetable plot. Others, such as globe artichokes, have decorative foliage, and bright red tomatoes are as nice to look at as they are good to eat. As a matter of fact, tomatoes were originally grown just for their decorative qualities; it was believed that the fruit was poisonous.

Herbs in particular can be grown in either the vegetable or flower garden, or used as a link between the two. Gardens specifically devoted to herbs are a fine romantic notion but are very difficult to execute in an effective way. They need a lot of attention and if this is lacking, they seem to get in a mess very quickly. It is much better to spread the herbs among the vegetables or flowers, both from the practical companionship point of view as well as for appearance sake.

LEFT *Tall madonna lilies* (Lilium candidum) *form a decorative background to two different colored forms of spinach beet and lettuces. The* Antirrhinum *in the foreground self-sow themselves through the vegetables and other flowering plants.*

BELOW *Parsley* (Petroselinum crispum) *grows luxuriantly in a flower border with annual zinnias* (Zinnia elegans) *and the tender shrub, rose periwinkle* (Catharanthus roseus).

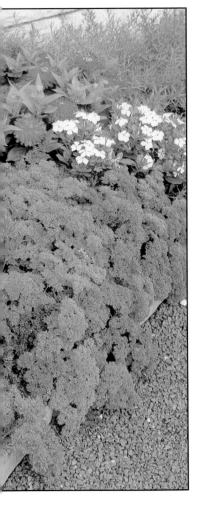

ABOVE *Here is a well-mixed border of petunias* (Petunia), *brassicas, lettuce, beans, and tomatoes, with little wasted space or room for weeds to grow. This is an attractive as well as productive border. The petunias may also help to repel a number of pests, including bean beetles.*

NATURE'S POLLINATORS

*T*here are very few gardens that are without charming bees and butterflies, even if they do not contain plants that bees and butterflies are particularly attracted to.

When bees are encouraged the air can positively hum with their busy activity. There are two main reasons for encouraging bees in a garden: the pollination service they run and the honey they provide (if you have hives). Many people have a third reason for wanting bees about: they add the dimension of noise to a garden already full of visual delights, pleasant scents, and tasty harvests.

This may seem fanciful, but the steady drone of the bees produces a soothing atmosphere next to none when it comes to relaxing. The pure sight of these busy little creatures also gives many people a great deal of delight.

The main purpose of bees, and, to a lesser extent, butterflies, in the garden is to provide pollination. Bees are particularly good pollinators because unlike other insects, they are selective in what flowering plants they visit. If, for example, clover is in flower and it is the most abundant nearby flower, bees will most naturally move from clover flower to clover flower, rather than moving

BEE-ATTRACTING PLANTS

Many insects, including flies, pollinate plants, but the bee is the most important pollinator. They are attracted to plants because of their nectar, but it is the pollen that accidentally attaches itself to their bodies that effects the pollination of plants.

Bee balm *Monarda didyma*
Blackberry *Rubus*
Borage *Borago officinalis*
Butterfly bush *Buddleia davidii*
Catmint *Nepeta*
Cherry *Prunus*
Chive *Allium schoenoprasum*
Clover *Trifolium*
Cotoneaster *Cotoneaster*
Crocus *Crocus*
Eucalyptus *Eucalyptus*
Fennel *Foeniculum vulgare*
Forget-me-not *Myosotis*
Globe flower *Echinops ritro*
Goldenrod *Solidago*

Hawthorn, or quick thorn *Crataegus*
Heather *Erica*
Hemp agrimony *Eupatorium*
Ivy *Hedera helix*
Lavender *Lavandula*
Lime *Tillia × europea*
Ling *Calluna vulgaris*
Marsh marigold *Caltha palustris*
Michaelmas daisy *Aster novi-belgii*
Mint *Mentha*
Marjoram *Origanum*
Poached-egg flower *Limnanthes douglasii*
Rosemary *Rosmarinus officinalis*
Stonecrop *Sedum*
Thyme *Thymus*

Its body dusted with pollen, a honey bee drinks deep from the nectar in this flower.

LEFT *Herb gardens are very evocative places in their own right, but the sound and movement of bees buzzing about intensifies this feeling. The herb garden makes an ideal place for the beehive, although the traditional one in the picture is more decorative than functional.*

on to another type of plant. This selectivity is important for good pollination, since plants must pollinate with plants of the same species.

Some plants are self-pollinating and need no help; others, particularly winter-flowering species which appear when there are few insects about, are wind-pollinated; but by far the great majority are insect-pollinated. Pollination is particularly important for vegetables where the very *raison d'être* of growing them is to produce the food they bear, and unless the flowers are pollinated the food will not form. It is not quite so important in the flower garden, but even here it is necessary if berries and fruit are desired for fall color, or if seed is needed for sowing the following year.

When planting fruit trees it is essential in many cases to give them companions. They will not pollinate with their own kind but need another variety with which to cross-pollinate. Care must be taken to ensure that any companions flower at the same time, otherwise cross-pollination cannot be effected. This includes apples (*Malus*), pears (*Pyrus*), and cherries (*Prunus avium*), but there are some plum (*Prunus domestica*) varieties which are self-fertile.

If you want honey, then you will have to keep hives and buy honey bees (or catch a swarm of them). It is doubtful if any normal-sized garden could provide enough flowering plants to keep a hive going, but bees will forage for up to 2 miles (3km), bringing back pollen and nectar from well beyond your own boundaries.

There are many plants that attract bees, butterflies, and, if you live in one of the Americas, the lovely hummingbird, the smallest bird in the world. If you are to have a truly companionable garden, then you should have at least a few of these plants.

Bees are naturally attracted to flowers, but there are a few that they find particularly alluring. These include forget-me-not (*Myosotis*), globe flower (*Echinops ritro*), goldenrod (*Solidago*), heather (*Erica*), lavender (*Lavandula*), and Michaelmas daisy (*Aster novi-belgii*).

Clover (*Trifolium*) is one of bees' favorite plants and will surely bring bees to your garden when it is in flower. You will get a double benefit from clover if you sow it into your lawn. It will attract bees and, because clover is a nitrogen-fixing legume, it will make nitrogen from the air available to the grass.

It is not only bees and other insects that pollinate plants. The wind is a very effective pollinator, particularly of grasses and those plants that flower too early in the year for there to be many insects about. Some of the strangest pollinators are slugs, but they are not, as far as is known, pollinators of garden plants. On the other hand, probably the most attractive and fascinating pollinators are the tiny hummingbirds, which eat half their weight in nectar each day. Their beautiful colors and vibrating wings make them a delight to watch in their native North America.

Although butterflies are pollinators, they are most appreciated in the garden for their lovely appearance. There are a number of plants that produce nectar that attracts these beautiful insects. Buddleia (above) and stonecrop (Sedum) (left), especially the later flowering forms, are both commonly seen covered with butterflies.

CHAPTER FIVE

EXOTIC COMPANIONS

Creating a microclimate in which exotic plants can live is not only beneficial to the plants, it can also result in a visually striking plant grouping. Opposite is a collection of epiphytic plants growing on dead branches that form the base of a humid jungle planting in a conservatory.

PLANTS THAT DEPEND UPON OTHERS

Air plants and bromeliads, growing on dead tree trunks and logs with other exotic plants such as orchids growing in the leafmold and peat of the forest floor, make exciting companions.

BROMELIAD PANELS

Air plants can make attractive wall decorations by mounting them on panels of wood. A cushion of sphagnum moss is placed between the base of the bromeliad and the panel, securing both with lengths of plastic-coated wire. They are best hung in a humid atmosphere. This is a particularly good way of displaying staghorn fern as seen here.

EXOTICA

Indoor companionship allows you to grow plants that are not generally seen outside the tropics. For example, there are many exotic orchids or fruiting plants and their relatives, such as the pineapple, (*Ananas*), seen above. This is an exciting field to explore, allowing gardening to continue throughout the year.

AIR PLANTS IN GREENHOUSES

Bromeliads can be grown in greenhouses or conservatories. The plants can be grown in pots on benches, or a more decorative approach can be made by creating raised beds to emulate miniature rain forests. Here the plants can be displayed to their best advantage, with several different species, as seen above, occupying one tree.

BROMELIAD TREES

Choose an old branch from a tree with a main stem and several side branches. To keep it steady give it a base made by putting the lower end into a pot of wet cement. Artificial branches can be made by wrapping natural cork around a wire netting former which has been stuffed with moisture-retentive foam.

Remove the plants from their pots, wrap the root balls in wet sphagnum, and tie with plastic-coated wire to the branches. Choose natural-looking positions on the branches for the plants, such as forks in the branches or where the stem flattens out. Keep the sphagnum moist by spraying it with water. *Tillandsia* are some of the best plants for decorating a bromeliad tree.

MINIATURE RAIN FORESTS

It is possible to devote part of your conservatory or greenhouse to a permanent bed for air plants, or epiphytes, and orchids. A bed can be created by building a frame of brick, blocks, or wood about 9–10in (23–25cm) deep. Drainage material such as gravel is put in the bottom and then the rest is filled with a 50/50 mixture of sharp sand and peat moss. Some dead branches can be permanently bedded into this (they might require cement bases to hold them steady). Other pieces of wood can be laid on the surface of the beds to look like stumps or fallen trees. These can all be planted with air plants and orchids, and more can be planted directly into the bed below. Ferns and other exotic plants can be added to the bed. Keep the soil moist but not overwatered. The air should be buoyant but not drafty.

brick frame

sharp sand and peat moss

gravel

PARASITIC PLANTS

There are some plants that have taken their companionship with other plants to extremes; they have become dependent on them for part or whole of their food supply. These plants are called parasitic plants. The best-known example of this is the mistletoe.

There are many species of *Viscum*, but it is the common mistletoe (*V. album*) that we all know. This is a green-leaved plant that forms a bushy outgrowth on the branches of its host tree or shrub. The flowers are insignificant, but it is the white, sticky berries that are one of the plant's main attractions. Mistletoe has green leaves and can manufacture some of its own food, but it is still dependent on the tree on which it grows; it cannot survive on its own. The most commonly seen host is the apple tree (*Malus*), but it also grows on hawthorn, or quick thorn (*Crataegus*), lime (*Tillia*), poplar (*Populus*), and some maples (*Acer*).

Birds commonly sow the mistletoe around the countryside. They eat the berry and then pass the seed through their gut. Because the seed is covered with a sticky substance from the birds' stomachs, it adheres to almost anything it lands upon. If it lands on and sticks to a tree branch, the seed puts out roots into the branch and a new plant is formed.

Mistletoe is not the only parasite of interest to gardeners. There are many others. Some plants, like the broomrape (*Orobanche*) have no chlorophyll in their leaves and are entirely dependent on their host plants for food. The Indian paintbrush, *Castilleja*, for example, is a particularly attractive genus of American plants. Like many parasites it is very difficult to grow and offers a challenge to gardeners.

Not all parasitic plants live off green living plants. There is a group called saprophytes which live on decaying organic matter and another, larger group which is dependent on mycorrhizal associations.

The saprophytes need not detain us here, as few are grown in gardens with the notable exception of mushrooms. It is mainly bacteria and fungi that live on

*Mistletoe (*Viscum album*) is one of the best-known of the parasitic plants. It is entirely dependent on its host and cannot grow without it. Its unusual dependency has, over the centuries, imbued it with all kinds of myths and folklore.*

There are several semi-parasitic plants that are dependent on their hosts. These can sometimes be grown on their own when they will support each other. The broomrapes (Orobanche) (left), are typical European examples, and the beautiful Indian paintbrushes (Castilleja) (above), are colorful examples from North America.

decaying material. These help in the food chain by breaking material down into a form that is usable by other plants. The most familiar manifestations of this are within the compost heap and the breakdown of leaf litter on the forest floor; both important processes for the gardener. There are a few flowering plants that live on this type of material, but they are devoid of chlorophyll and of little garden value. Out of interest it might be worth mentioning a couple of examples: the birds-nest orchid (*Neottia nidus-avis*) from Britain and the Indian pipe (*Monotropa uniflora*) and candy stick (*Allotropa virgata*), both from the United States.

Mycorrhizal association, in spite of it being a mouthful to say, is important to the gardener. This is an association between cells in the roots of plants and the threadlike mycelia or "roots" of fungus. Many plants have this form of relationship but in some it is more important than others. For example, many terrestrial orchids cannot grow without a mycorrhizal association. This makes them very difficult to cultivate unless certain fungi are present in the soil, making it a challenge to the gardener. Sometimes plants will not grow or flower in one part of the garden and yet when moved to a similar position elsewhere will flower perfectly. This often has to do with the plant's underground associations.

Another aspect of mycorrhizal association that could be important for the future is that the fungal mycelia form threadlike links between the roots of different plants. It is already known that disease can be transmitted between plants through this link. Since chemicals can be moved from plant to plant in this way, it may be that they are similarly able to transmit poisonous compounds, and it is just possible that strains will be created which can naturally kill off certain types of neighboring weeds. Many seed coatings naturally give off chemicals to inhibit growth of their neighbors in order to give them a head start in germination. It is not too fanciful to see this being developed into something with greater implications sometime in the future.

Dactylorhiza majalis *is typical of the plants that need mycorrhizal association. It is one of the easiest orchids to* grow in the open garden and, *once established in a supportive environment, it will form quite large colonies.*

Monotropa hypopitus *(above) is a saprophyte living on dead plant material. It is not exactly an eye-catching plant, but may be just the thing for gardeners who like curiosities.*

Cypripediums (left), like all terrestial orchids, need a mycorrhizal association. They are attractive orchids that are occasionally available from specialist nurseries.

AIR PLANTS

Air plants, or epiphytes, are not new to many gardeners, but they are becoming increasingly popular as more is understood about their culture, and as more of these plants are available to the gardening public.

An epiphyte is a plant that grows on another plant but gains no nourishment from it. The most common examples of these are ferns, mosses, and lichens which grow quite readily in shrubs and trees. Tropical areas, where high humidity and warm temperatures are constant all year round, contain the most epiphytes. The colorful and exotic tree orchid is a typical example.

These plants are only dependent on their hosts for support. They gather their nutrients from decaying organic material that naturally collects around them, and the water they need is provided by the rainfall or extracted from the humid air (hence the name air plants). Roots are produced but these are just for holding the plant stable on its host. The strange ways in which they get their food and water have led to their many unusual structures and forms, often quite unlike their terrestrial equivalents. Allied to this is their often bizarre coloring. Their curious shapes and colors are making epiphytes a very popular group of plants to grow.

In colder areas host epiphytes (with the exception of mosses and lichens) have to be grown under glass, but in warmer climates it is possible to grow them outside as long as the moisture they need can be maintained. They can be grown in pots but look better if grown on real branches of trees or on artificial ones made from wire and cork (see pages 130-131). They are tropical plants in the main and prefer a humid situation. Spray the plants to keep them moist and see that the central "vase" of the flower is kept filled with water.

LEFT *Here are natural epiphytic companions: polypody ferns and moss growing together on an old oak (*Quercus*) tree. The clean, humid woodland air creates ideal conditions for these to grow together.*

ABOVE *A companionable jungle forms a microclimate in a conservatory, with epiphytes growing on carefully positioned tree trunks. Here* Tillandsia usneoides *cascades like water from the dead branches.*

SOME BROMELIADS
TO TRY

Bromeliads are available in a wide range of exotic shapes and colors. They can be grown singly in pots but are happier grown on wood and in the company of other plants. The majority need warmth and humidity and prefer greenhouse conditions.

Aechmea fasciata

Ananas comosus

Billbergia porteana

Cryptanthus acaulis 'Rubra'

Guzmania linguata

Neoregelia spectabilis

Nidularium billbergioides

Tillandsia lindeniana

Vriesea poetmannii

137

GLOSSARY

Acid soil Soil with little or no lime content, having a pH level of 6.5 or less.

Air plants Also known as epiphytes, plants that physically grow on other plants, often trees, but are not dependent on them for nourishment.

Alkaline soil Soil with a high lime content, having a pH value of more than 7.4.

Alleopathy The process whereby a plant restricts the growth or development of other plants around it by releasing toxic chemicals.

Alternative hosts Also referred to as decoy plants, these are plants that are used to attract insect pests away from the principal crop.

Beneficial insects Those insects that are helpful to the gardener because they pollinate plants or prey on pests.

Broadcasting The scattering of seed over an area, as opposed to sowing it in drills.

Calcifuge A plant that dislikes alkaline soil.

Chlorophyll The green pigment found in plants' leaves and stems.

Climbing plants Tall, spindly plants that need the support of other plants, a fence or trellis.

Clone A group of identical plants that have been vegetatively propagated from the same source.

Companion plants Plants that relate in a positive way to their neighbouring plants.

Compost Organic material like garden and kitchen wastes that has decomposed to form a nutrient-rich humus.

Cover crops Crops that are planted to protect the ground between the harvest of one main crop and the sowing of the next.

Cultivar A variety of a plant originating in cultivation as opposed to in the wild.

Cutting A piece of stem cut away from a plant to be rooted in order to produce a new plant.

Dioecious Having male and female flowers on separate plants. Both male and female plants are required for pollination.

Division Method of propagation in which the plant is split into several parts so that each part can grow into a separate new plant.

Dormancy A period when a plant or a seed is inactive and waiting for some stimulus to start it into growth.

Double digging Breaking up the soil to the depth of two spades.

Drills Shallow trenches drawn out for sowing seeds.

Earthing up The drawing up of earth around a plant. Especially done to potatoes and celery.

Epiphytes *See* Air plants.

Evergreen A plant that does not lose its leaves but has them all year round.

Farmyard manure Manure produced by cattle, horses, chickens, etc. For safe use in the garden it must be well-rotted or composted thoroughly.

Fastigiate Having branches that grow almost vertically, parallel to the trunk, having a columnar outline.

Focal point A point to which the eye is drawn.

Friable soil Soil that is crumbly in texture.

Frost hollows An area where the cold air that causes frosts gathers. Also known as frost pockets.

Genus A grouping of plants having similar characteristics. It is subdivided into species and is represented by the first element in a botanical name.

Germination The first stage in the development and growth of a seed.

Glaucous Covered in a bluish bloom.

Green manure Plants grown so that they can then be dug directly into the soil, while they are still green, in order to enrich it.

Ground cover Plants grown not necessarily for their harvest but to cover large areas of soil when the garden or field is idle. They are often planted to keep weeds down and prevent soil erosion.

Herbicides Chemicals used to kill off vegetation, in particular weeds.

Hosts Plants that attract insects because they are a good source of nectar, pollen, or other food.

Humus Decayed organic matter such as leafmold, garden compost, or farmyard manure.

Hybrid A plant created by crossing two dissimilar parent plants.

Insecticides Chemicals used to combat insect pests.

Intercropping Growing two or more crops together to make the best use of the ground available or because of the mutual benefit they afford each other. Also known as interplanting.

Jardin potager A French kitchen garden, usually with the vegetables planted decoratively, often within low hedge borders.

Leafmold Partially decayed leaves, useful for incorporating into the soil as humus.

Leguminous plants Plants belonging to the pea family. Valuable for their ability to fix nitrogen from the air into the soil, thereby making it available to other plants.

Monocrops Crops of a single variety filling the whole of the garden or plot.

Mulch A cover of organic material placed around the plant primarily to help retain moisture in the soil and to restrict the growth of weeds.

Neutral soil Soil that is neither acid nor alkaline, having a pH of 7.0.

pH A scale used for showing the degree of alkalinity or acidity of the soil.

Parasites Plants that grow on other plants on which they are dependent for food and support.

Plant association The way plants relate to other plants.

Pollination The fertilization of a flower by the transfer of pollen from male to female parts.

Predators Insects that eat other insects.

Propagation The means of increasing the numbers of a plant.

Prostrate Close to the ground, low growing.

Rotation of crops The yearly movement of crops from one place in the garden to another to make the best use of the ground and to reduce the incidence of pests and diseases.

Saprophytes Plants that live on the dead remains of other plants.

Soil erosion The washing or blowing away of soil by winds, rains, and floods.

Soil sickness A disease caused by repeatedly growing the same crop in the same soil.

Species An individual or closely related group of plants within a genus.

Successional cropping The planting of a new crop as soon as one is harvested so that the ground is always in use.

Successional planting The positioning of plants in a garden so that one takes its place visually as the other dies back.

Sucker A shoot other than the main stem that produces a new plant when it grows to the soil surface.

Tender Plants unable to withstand frosts.

Thinning The process of reducing the number of seedlings in a row so that the remaining ones have room to grow.

Tilth The physical condition of the surface of the soil. A fine tilth is needed for sowing seeds.

Variety Any distinct form of species or hybrid.

Vegetative propagation Propagation by methods other than seed. Produces a plant identical to its parent.

INDEX

CREDITS

Every effort has been made to obtain copyright clearance, and we do apologize if any omissions have been made. The author and Quarto would like to thank the following organizations for their co-operation.

p2 The Garden Picture Library; **p4** S & O Mathews; **p8** The Garden Picture Library; **pp10-11** The Garden Picture Library; **p12** S & O Mathews; **p13** *left:* James Austin; *right:* courtesy Burpee's seeds; **p14** *above:* Douglas Dickins; *below:* S & O Mathews; **p15** Eddie Ryle-Hodges; **p16** Harry Smith Collection; **p18** The Henry Doubleday Research Association; **p19** A-Z Botanical Collection; **p21** Eddie Ryle-Hodges; **p22** Photos Horticultural; **p24** Eddie Ryle-Hodges; **p26** Derek Fell; **p27** *left:* Harry Smith Collection; *right:* S & O Mathews; **p28** Photos Horticultural; **p29** Derek Fell; **p31** Harry Smith Collection; **p32** Photos Horticultural; **p34** The Garden Picture Library; **p36** *above:* Robert Opie; *below:* Quarto; **p37** The Garden Picture Library; **p42** Photos Horticultural; **p43** Iris Hardwick Library; **p44** Eddie Ryle-Hodges; **p48** Derek Fell; **p49** The Garden Picture Library; **p50** A-Z Botanical Collection; **p51** *above:* Photos Horticultural; *middle, left:* Frank Lane Picture Agency; *middle, right:* Oxford Scientific Films; *below:* Frank Lane Picture Agency; **p52** Photos Horticultural; **p53** Derek Fell; **pp54-55** Derek Fell; **p56** *top:* Oxford Scientific Films; *middle, from left:* Oxford Scientific Films; Frank Lane Picture Agency; Oxford Scientific Films; **pp60-61** Oxford Scientific Films; **p63** Derek Fell; **p64** Jerry Howard Positive Images; **p66** Harry Smith Collection; **p67** Derek Fell; **p68** Photos Horticultural; **p69** S & O Mathews; **p71** *left:* The Henry Doubleday Research Association; *right:* The Garden Picture Library; **p73** Photos Horticultural; **p75** The Garden Picture Library; **p76** S & O Mathews; **p78** Cynthia Woodyard; **p79** S & O Mathews; **p80** Photos Horticultural; **p81** The Garden Picture Library; **p83** S & O Mathews; **p84** A-Z Botanical Collection; **p85** *top, left:* Derek Fell; *top, right:* Harry Smith Collection; *bottom, left:* Derek Fell; *bottom, right:* Jerry Howard Positive Images; **p86** Derek Fell; **p87** *left:* Harry Smith Collection; *right:* S & O Mathews; **p89** Derek Fell; **p90** Harry Smith Collection; **p91** Photos Horticultural; **p92** Derek Fell; **p93** The Garden Picture Library; **p94** Cynthia Woodyard; **p95** Harry Smith Collection; **p96** Photos Horticultural; **p97** Harry Smith Collection; **p98** Derek Fell; **p99** *above:* Margaret Henzel Positive Images; *below:* Moira Clinch; **p100** S & O Mathews; **p101** Derek Fell; **p102** Derek Fell; **p103** *left:* Margaret Henzel Positive Images; *right:* S & O Mathews; **p112** S & O Mathews; **p115** *left:* Photos Horticultural; *right:* Harry Smith Collection; **p116** The Garden Picture Library; **p118** Harry Smith Collection; **p119** Derek Fell; **p120** S & O Mathews; **p121** *above:* Photos Horticultural; *below:* Derek Fell; **pp122-123** Derek Fell; **p124** Derek Fell; **p125** Frank Lane Picture Agency; **p126** Frank Lane Picture Agency; **p127** *above:* Harry Smith Collection; *below:* Photos Horticultural; **p128** Photos Horticultural; **p130** *left:* Harry Smith Collection; *right:* A-Z Botanical Collection; **p131** Harry Smith Collection; **p132** Photos Horticultural; **p133** *left:* Harry Smith Collection; *right:* A-Z Botanical Collection; **p134** S & O Mathews; **p135** Harry Smith Collection; **p136** *left:* A-Z Botanical Collection; *right:* Harry Smith Collection; **p137** A-Z Botanical Collection.